If reading your Bible feels dry and heavy, *The Well-Watered Woman* will bring back your passion to connect with Jesus. Nothing on earth is more important than loving and enjoying God through his Word.

JENNIE ALLEN
New York Times bestselling author of *Get Out of Your Head*; founder and visionary of IF:Gathering

Over the years, Gretchen has been a gift to us. Her honesty, vulnerability, and commitment to follow Christ in life and ministry have encouraged us in our own. *The Well-Watered Woman* is an overflow of Gretchen's life and a new beginning for any soul that feels barren, parched, or unsatisfied. Gretchen's story and words will cause you to love God more and will stir your affections for him.

EMILY JENSEN AND LAURA WIFLER
Coauthors of *Risen Motherhood: Gospel Hope for Everyday Moments*; cofounders of the Risen Motherhood ministry

We all know that beautiful, flourishing gardens—and lives—don't just happen. Gretchen combines rich, biblical insight with transparent glimpses into her own journey to help dry, parched souls become thriving, life-giving springs. You will find great hope and encouragement in this book as you encounter Jesus in a fresh way.

NANCY DEMOSS WOLGEMUTH
Author and founder/teacher of *Revive Our Hearts*

Gretchen offers a fresh perspective on living a faith-filled life that both revives the dried-up Christian's hope and lets her breathe a sigh of relief. She gives her readers permission to ditch the pursuit of picture-perfect spiritual performance and, instead, embrace authenticity with God so that his presence and his Word can flow down and water the parched, untouched roots of her weary soul.

TITANIA PAIGE
Host of *The Purpose in Purity Podcast* and author of *Come Home: A Redemptive Roadmap from Lust Back to Christ*

If you're weary of the try-harder, do-more, be-better pressures of daily life, don't miss Gretchen Saffles's new book. Gretchen writes with warmth and humility, graciously illuminating our need for the Good News of the gospel. This book overflows with scriptural truths that will refresh your heart, nourish your soul, and point you to Jesus.

MELISSA KRUGER
Director of Women's Initiatives for The Gospel Coalition and author of *Growing Together: Taking Mentoring Beyond Small Talk and Prayer Requests*

As a pastor, I am always looking for resources to help our women grow in Christ. This book both helps women understand their own past, fears, and ungodly desires and offers them a gospel-centered approach to real Christian growth. The illustration comparing growing plants to the Christian life that Gretchen weaves throughout the book is so helpful for every reader, from someone who is just getting to know Christ to a mature follower. I can't wait to recommend this book to every woman in my church, with the great hope that it will help each one become a more Well-Watered Woman.

DR. JASON EDWIN DEES
Pastor, Christ Covenant, Atlanta, Georgia

Whether we realize it or not, we are constantly looking in the wrong places to find satisfaction. This book is an invitation to run to the only Well that will fulfill the deepest longings of our hearts. Gretchen saturated these pages with biblical truth that will revive you! Come thirsty, and expect to be refreshed!

BETSEY GOMEZ
Podcaster, Revive Our Hearts Spanish Outreach

Gretchen Saffles doesn't only teach what it means to be a Well-Watered Woman. She lives it. She isn't perfect, and she'll share her struggles throughout her book. But as you get to know Gretchen, more importantly, you'll get to know Jesus. She desires to be filled each day with God's Word because it is living, active, and profitable for our daily lives. The best part is that her delight in God's Word will splash on you, leaving you refreshed and renewed to trust in the God who redeems and refreshes our souls.

KELLY KING
Manager of Magazines/Devotional Publishing and Women's Ministry Training, Lifeway Christian Resources

The Well-Watered Woman stirred my affections for Jesus and reminded me that following him is a lifestyle, not merely a box to check off on my spiritual to-do list. In this book, Gretchen Saffles points to Christ on every page and, in doing so, invites readers to look to him every moment of every day.

HUNTER BELESS
Founder and executive director of Journeywomen

It takes time for things to grow. Growth in the Christian life is a process too. This book helps define a process of growth, but more important, it helps you see that the destination is not the process but a Person. If you would describe your soul as dry, parched, and in need of water, this book is for you. Even if you are in a great place spiritually, this book will encourage you to keep fighting the fight and living by faith. He is worthy and worth it!

JULIE WOODRUFF
Women's minister, Long Hollow Baptist Church

With gentle words of encouragement and truth, Gretchen takes readers by the hand and leads them on a journey from thirsting for the truth to seeking satisfaction in the Well of God's Word. She has truly walked this journey with humility and has led us all in displaying the testimony of her life with honest vulnerability. Her kindness in coming alongside women brings hope and healing to anyone who is tired of the try-harder life and longs for abundance in Christ alone.

JESSICA MATHISEN
Author of *Already Chosen*

Every season of life has its challenges, but *The Well-Watered Woman* points us to the God of all seasons. With transparent examples from her own life story, Gretchen encourages readers that the Word of God is necessary for our roots to run deep, and she reminds us that joy is only possible through Jesus. Whether you are in a fruitful or dry season, this book directs you to the true Well we must draw from.

DIANNE JAGO
Author of *A Holy Pursuit: How the Gospel Frees Us to Follow and Lay Down Our Dreams*; founder of Deeply Rooted Magazine

Worn out? Burned out? Desperate for real hope and strength? This book is a lifeline for a generation of women who are experiencing anxiety, burnout, and weariness at record levels. I urgently want to put this gorgeous and timely book into the hands of every Christian woman I know. Don't miss this one.

JENNIFER DUKES LEE
Author of *Growing Slow* and *It's All Under Control*

I'm convinced every woman will find herself on these pages as Gretchen opens our eyes to the reason we feel so dry and tired. If you're thirsty and longing to feel the quench that lasts for more than an episode of your favorite show, pick up this book and be reminded of the everlasting and refreshing hope of the gospel.

VALERIE WOERNER
Owner and creator of Val Marie Paper prayer journals and author of *Grumpy Mom Takes a Holiday*

My time with Jesus in the Word is a nonnegotiable in my life. It's the only way I make it through my day with peace and joy. Yet I know many Christian women feel defeated and discouraged in this area of their life. They know they "should" be reading their Bibles, they "should" be praying, but they just can't seem to overcome the stress, guilt, and anxiety bearing down on them. What a gift of grace this book will be for them and every weary soul that picks it up! In *The Well-Watered Woman*, Gretchen has laid out a compelling and grace-filled vision for a thriving life, one with Jesus at the center. Each chapter is an invitation to find refreshment at the Well, rest in the Word, and purpose in the Way. These simple and profound truths are not burdensome or overwhelming but, rather, simple and strong enough to implement immediately into everyday life. In this book, you'll find refreshment for your soul and the tools to stay that way.

KELLY NEEDHAM
Author of *Friendish: Reclaiming Real Friendship in a Culture of Confusion*

I found myself worshiping the Lord as I was reading these beautiful, truth-filled pages! Gretchen has written the book the world needs right now—an invitation to bloom where we've been planted. *The Well-Watered Woman* is balm for our souls, leading us to drink at the Well that never runs dry. This book will refresh, renew, and ready you for life to the full, right where you are!

LARA CASEY
Bestselling author of *Make it Happen*, *Cultivate*, and *Gracie's Garden*

For every woman who feels thirsty and dry and a little bit empty, *The Well-Watered Woman* offers a taste of Living Water from a Well that will never run dry. Through her own transparent journey, Gretchen points us to Jesus and the life-giving relationship he longs to have with every one of us. So grateful for this beautiful book!

JOANNA WEAVER
Bestselling author of *Having a Mary Heart in a Martha World: Finding Intimacy with God in the Busyness of Life*

For the woman who is dried up, worn out, and barely holding on, *The Well-Watered Woman* speaks directly to the core. Gretchen's personal story of letting Christ grow her up, expand her roots, and satisfy her soul will inspire readers to let God do the same in their own hearts. If you're ready to truly experience the gospel's promise, this book is for you.

PHYLICIA MASONHEIMER
National bestselling author of *Stop Calling Me Beautiful*

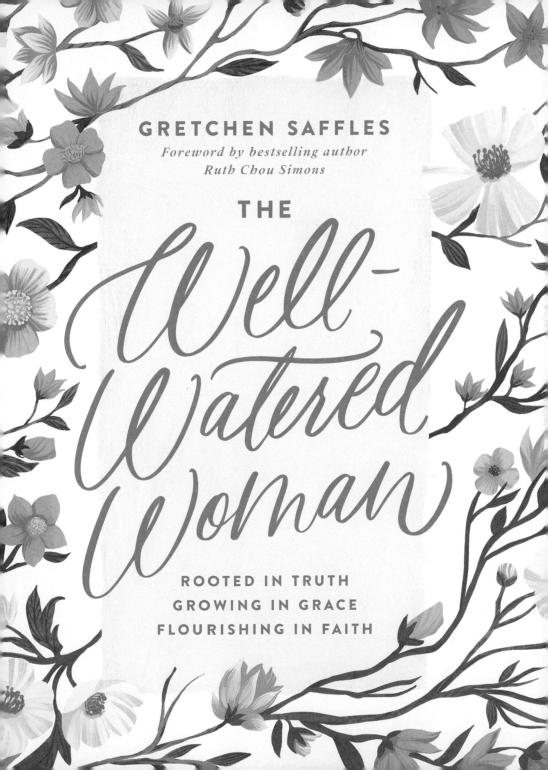

GRETCHEN SAFFLES

Foreword by bestselling author
Ruth Chou Simons

THE
Well-Watered Woman

ROOTED IN TRUTH
GROWING IN GRACE
FLOURISHING IN FAITH

Visit Tyndale online at tyndale.com.

Visit Tyndale Momentum online at tyndalemomentum.com.

Visit the author's website at wellwateredwomen.com.

TYNDALE, Tyndale's quill logo, *Tyndale Momentum*, and the Tyndale Momentum logo are registered trademarks of Tyndale House Ministries. Tyndale Momentum is the nonfiction imprint of Tyndale House Publishers, Carol Stream, Illinois.

The Well-Watered Woman: Rooted in Truth, Growing in Grace, Flourishing in Faith

Designed by Libby Dykstra

Edited by Stephanie Rische

Published in association with William K. Jensen Literary Agency, 119 Bampton Court, Eugene, Oregon 97404.

For information about special discounts for bulk purchases, please contact Tyndale House Publishers at csresponse@tyndale.com, or call 1-800-323-9400.

ISBN 978-1-4964-4545-2

Printed in China

28   27   26   25   24
11   10   9   8   7

To Well-Watered Women around the world:
You are the hands and feet of Jesus—
and the reason I wrote this book.
Keep bringing him your nothing,
receiving his everything,
and sharing it with the world.

And to my mama, who has lived this message
faithfully right before my eyes—
through suffering and sorrow,
through joy and every tomorrow.
You are God's gift of grace to me.
You are the Well-Watered Woman.

CONTENTS

FOREWORD

I used to think I was the only one who struggled to read my Bible.

I'd look at godly women I admired but didn't know personally and fill in my own narrative of what it must be like to have her vibrant relationship with God:

She must spend three hours a day studying her Bible.
I bet she has memorized long sections of Scripture.
Her kids don't fuss and fight while she's trying to read her Bible.
She probably doesn't get distracted like I do.
How does she get so much out of the Bible?
Something must be wrong with me.

Isn't it just like the enemy to derail us from the prize of knowing Jesus with the mirage of "doing it right"? When people learn that I paint Scripture and write for Christian women, they always assume that spending time in the Word comes easily or naturally for me. They imagine me sitting on the back porch, lingering luxuriously with my Bible and commentaries open—while birds chirp, worship songs play, and a paintbrush loaded with fresh watercolor paint waits at the ready in case I get inspired. And sometimes they are right (perhaps once or twice a year). But most days, time with God and his Word looks more like this:

Rubbing the tired out of my eyes, praying first for desire (and confessing my lack), opening my Bible only to set it down to work through a disruption from the kids, returning once again, jotting down some notes, underlining a passage I don't understand, putting the dog out (again), and coming back to it several hours later, forgetting where I started that morning.

Some days . . . some seasons . . . are just not visibly flush with flashy and fragrant blooms.

Years ago, while watering my not-yet-blooming plants on the windowsill, I jotted down these words that formed in my heart: You don't have to be blooming to be growing. I was in an achy growing season—one that felt endlessly filled with weeding, pruning, watering, cultivating. And not many blooms.

It was in that season that the Lord taught me to long for him more than productivity. He showed me the richness of his provision when I wanted quick results. He stilled my heart with reminders of my identity in Christ when I thought I needed to secure my identity elsewhere. He opened my eyes to his faithfulness even in my faithlessness. God grew me in the midst of a non-blooming season by instructing me through his Word.

It was around that same season that Gretchen and I first met each other online. Though it was years before we met in person, we knew we were kindred sisters in the Lord, eager to use our gifts and talents to direct many hearts back to Christ. We're both creatives, watching for ways God declares his glory and draws us to himself through beauty, creation, and his Word.

For years, I've watched Gretchen lead and lean into the mission of encouraging women to dig deeply into the Word of God. I've seen her model this, share vulnerably through difficult seasons, and consistently point others to God's faithfulness. God has written a story in and through her that is not about her but about God's tending and care. And through these pages, Gretchen leads us again and again back to the only source for life and godliness—the living water of God's Word.

The Bible isn't a formula, a quick fix, or a self-help strategy plan; it is a life-transforming love letter from the heart of God to you and me. In an age where so many seek to better themselves through worldly methods, we as Christ-followers must cling to this truth: "The grass withers, the flower fades, but the word of our God will stand forever" (Isaiah 40:8).

A soul anchored to the hope found in the life, death, and resurrection of Christ will always bloom where it's planted. That's my only hope. That is Gretchen's only hope. My prayer for you, as you begin this journey through the pages of this book, is that you, too, will find your hope in Christ—sustained by his Word, transformed into his likeness, and flourishing with fruitful blooms in due season—beginning right where you are.

RUTH CHOU SIMONS
Author of *GraceLaced* and *Beholding and Becoming*;
founder of GraceLaced.com

BEGINNING AT THE END

Life on Earth matters not because it's the only life we have, but precisely because it isn't—it's the beginning of a life that will continue without end.
RANDY ALCORN

She was precariously close to dying when I found her, holding on to her last gasps of life, limp from dehydration and neglect. It looked like revival was hopeless. I picked her up tenderly, rushing to the kitchen sink to get the water she needed. Only time would tell if my little plant would make it, so I began the wait.

I felt a pang of guilt as I glanced at the fallen, shriveled-up leaves. I'd placed my dainty speckled plant haphazardly in the corner of an upstairs room where the blinds often remained shut. I'd forgotten all about her as I rushed about my busy schedule—caring for my little ones, tending to my work, keeping up my home, and trying to survive the daily grind. In many ways, my life was like that plant when I found it on the brink

of death. As my little houseplant wilted from a lack of attention, light, and water, I was languishing too. On the outside, my
life looked like it was in order, but my soul wasn't getting the
care it needed. Anxiety lurked around every corner, and I found
myself facing fears and relentless what-ifs.

This wasn't the first time I'd found myself shriveling, dried
up, and wilting. My plant served as a poignant reminder that
the well-watered life doesn't happen by accident, and it doesn't
happen overnight either. Rather, the well-watered life must be
fought for, invested in, and tended to with love. It's the kind of life
we were created to live, and it's the kind of life Jesus came to give.

The work of God's redemption in our lives is a slow-moving
journey that takes place in mostly unseen ways. Growth is
rarely glamorous; instead, it's forged in the rocky hills of hardship, the valleys of suffering, and the foggy paths of waiting. It's
marked by a gradual movement toward Christ in the middle of
the messy, mundane moments of life. If you expect life to be
perfect, you will be let down every time. But if you embrace the
struggle, eyes glued to Jesus, you will surrender to your Savior
and find in him the perfection you long for. He's working in
your waiting, creating a masterpiece out of your mess. In other
words: life won't ever be easy, but God is always good.

WHEN YOU REACH THE END

Like my poor plant, you may have hit a spot in your life that
feels like an ending. There are no signs of hope, and revival

seems like a long shot at best. I don't know what your ending is—maybe it's the end of a season or the end of a relationship. Maybe you're facing what feels like a dead end, or you're at the crossroads of a decision you need to make. You may be nearing (or at) the end of your own abilities or resources or the end of a dream you once cherished. Or maybe you're at the end of your rope, wondering how God's goodness will prevail in the darkness of life.

But there's a hidden gift that comes with endings. With every ending comes a new beginning. When you reach the end, you're given a fresh opportunity to begin again. It's only when you reach your end, when you're dried up and shriveling, that you realize where real life comes from in the first place. We can never know the joy of flourishing without experiencing the despair of languishing. Apart from Jesus, we are spiritually dead, lifeless, overcome by the weeds of sin. But when we come to the end of ourselves, we can commit fully to Christ, and we can be made new and set free.

Every ending in my own life has brought about a new beginning that wouldn't have been possible without the closing of a previous chapter. The end of my pride brings humility. The end of jealousy brings love. The end of a season brings a new opportunity to see God's faithfulness. It's in these endings that true life begins. Every ending I've faced on earth isn't really the end of my story; it's the beginning of knowing Jesus more fully—an arrow pointing me to the hopeful end that's still to come.

And on a larger scale, the end of our time on earth means the best beginning of all. In the end, every wrong will be made right, every pain healed, every suffering redeemed, and every hardship relieved. Every tear will be wiped away, every question answered, every desert turned into a fruitful garden, and every broken heart mended (see Revelation 21:1-6). The end of the story is even better than the beginning, and it's full of hope.

So if you feel you're at your end, or nearing your end, you're actually in the perfect place. Because it's in your ending that you will find the perfect beginning in Christ.

FOR THE WOMAN WHO FEELS DRIED UP

I wrote this book for the woman who is in need of a fresh start. She feels discouraged by the lack of growth in her faith. She's tired of trying to prove herself and feels stuck in the mud of the mundane. She attends church but finds her Bible collecting dust on a shelf during the week. She wants to go deeper and love Jesus more, but she doesn't know *how* to move forward. She feels parched on the inside.

This book is for the woman who desires abundant life in Christ but also finds herself craving more of this world—more affirmation, more money, more accomplishments, more pleasure. She is hungry to embrace Christ's grace, but she struggles to live this out when her child is throwing a tantrum, when her roommate betrays her, when her coworker gossips about her, or when her emotions rage and throw their own tantrum.

I wrote this for the woman who has come to the end of her rope so many times that she's almost ready to let go. She finds herself trudging along on the hamster wheel of life, using up all her energy but getting nowhere. She doesn't know how to get from the dried-up life to the overflowing life Jesus offers.

I wrote this book for every woman who wants more of Jesus in her everyday life but struggles to live out this desire.

But I also wrote it for me because I am this woman. I'm the woman who has run tirelessly for a prize that's out of reach and ultimately unsatisfying. I'm the woman who has searched for meaning and purpose in what I can accomplish, only to be left empty handed. I'm the woman who is breathless and exhausted from chasing after perfection. I'm the woman who has tried drinking from an empty well, aching for living water while gulping down fear, anxiety, and panic.

I'm the dried-up woman.

THE WELL-WATERED WOMAN: WHO IS SHE?

I can pretty much guarantee none of us set out on a path to become shriveled up and at the end of ourselves. It happens gradually, and one day we're shocked to discover just how desperate and thirsty we are. I know this has been the case for me.

I grew up in the church, but in my early twenties, I found myself still unsure of what it looks like to follow Jesus in everyday life. I wanted more than just an "open your Bible once a week and then let it collect dust" kind of faith. The Jesus I read about in the Bible was either worth everything or worth nothing. Living as if he were only worth "something" just wouldn't cut it. I found myself craving not just a few drops of water every once in a while but a deep, soul-nourishing, life-giving stream.

I've learned that it's impossible to become a flourishing, deeply rooted woman simply by opening my Bible every so often. I can't expect to thrive when my thirsty soul is trying to sip from empty wells throughout the day, while the well of living water beckons me to come and drink the truth that satisfies forever. As my sad little plant reminds me, becoming a Well-Watered Woman isn't a goal I check off my to-do list once; rather, it's a way of life.

The Well-Watered Woman isn't the perfect woman. She's fueled by the undeserved grace of God, not by her ambitions to be a "good girl." She recognizes that the good within her comes from God alone (see Psalm 16:2; Galatians 5:22-23). Jesus has set her free from her past mistakes, and she lives as a new creation (see 2 Corinthians 5:17). He has given her a fresh start, and his mercy propels her forward in love and obedience each day. She has come to the end of herself and found a new beginning in Jesus. Her future is secure, and her new life is most hopeful of all—eternity with Christ.

The goal of the Well-Watered Woman isn't to *be* someone but to *know* someone—the one who changes everything. Her ambitions and dreams are being transformed by Jesus as he shows her, day by day, the better way to live. As she makes it her daily pursuit to know Jesus, she becomes the someone God created her to be: the Well-Watered Woman.

BRING YOUR EMPTY CUP

Ultimately, being "well watered" isn't just about getting adequate water; it's also about *where* it's coming from. If our thirst is temporarily satisfied by water from a polluted source, we won't grow and flourish even if the soil is wet. For the Well-Watered Woman, Jesus himself is the Well she drinks from daily. He's her source of hope, healing, peace, and purpose. He's the living water who satisfies the thirsty soul forever and fills her empty cup.

The Well-Watered Woman can't exist apart from God's grace. I know because I've tried. I used to attempt to fill my cup from the dried-up wells and empty promises of this world. I sought purpose and happiness in what I achieved, but no matter how hard I tried, it was never enough. I put all my energy into being liked by others, but they were never satisfied. I craved what this world has to offer, but it never provided peace. It was only when I looked to Jesus that I found the satisfaction I longed for.

The promise in Isaiah 58:11 changed everything for me. The first time I read this passage, it seemed too good to be true: "The LORD will guide you always; he will satisfy your needs in a sun-scorched land and will strengthen your frame. You will be like a well-watered garden, like a spring whose waters never fail" (NIV). This verse comes in the context of God calling the

Israelites from a dried-up life to a life of obedience and abundance in him.

At the time I read this, I was trudging through a dark night of the soul. On the outside, I looked like I had things together, but on the inside, I was drying up. I relied on the "good" I could find in myself rather than the goodness of God, and I was withering in a sun-scorched land.

But Jesus didn't leave me there. He opened my eyes, and I saw myself as the dried-up woman in John 4—the one who met Jesus at the well and received his offer of water from a Well that never dries up. This woman had been pursuing water from a temporary source, but that didn't stop Jesus from pursuing her. And it didn't stop him from pursuing me, either. He offered me living water just as he did for the woman at the well, and I haven't been the same since.

So if your cup is empty, you're in the right place. You have to know you're thirsty before you can drink from the Well that always satisfies and never runs dry.

IN SEARCH OF A GOOD ENDING

Throughout this book, we will go on a journey of growing in Christ—a journey toward the well-watered life. This book is broken down into three different sections that characterize the Well-Watered Woman: "The Well," "The Word," and "The Way."

"The Well" is the starting point, where the gospel is planted in your life and your roots take hold in the truth. It's here that your identity becomes grounded in the gospel—where you begin to grasp who God is and the reality of who you are in him. The soil of your soul will be cultivated so you can learn to be more than "okay" in Christ, what it means to die to yourself, and to find joy and purpose right where you're planted.

The next section, "The Word," represents growth in Christ. The Well-Watered Woman is *always* growing, changing, and being transformed into Jesus' likeness. Jesus, who is the Word, is our source for growth. You'll discover what it means to put the Word before the world, to stir your affections for Jesus, and to preach Truth with a capital *T* to your heart.

The last section, "The Way," represents blooming and flourishing in Christ. We'll look at how obedience and love for Jesus affect the way we think, act, and go about our daily life. This is where what has been planted and nurtured begins to produce fruit, the natural outcome of a well-watered life.

At the beginning of each chapter, you'll find "The Story of a Thirsty Woman." These stories are composites of real struggles we face as women. The details of your own story will vary, but I hope you will relate to the feelings at the core of these stories, because the dried-up woman is you, and she is me. We have all been dried up at some point, but Jesus doesn't want us to stay there. He came to offer us abundant life in him. By the end of each chapter, my hope is that you'll see how this woman (who represents all of us) can be transformed into the Well-Watered Woman as she finds her hope in Jesus.

YOUR FRESH START BEGINS *NOW*

Miraculously, less than twenty-four hours after I watered my neglected plant, it revived. As I type these words, she sits by an open window, upright, healthy, and growing. This plant was given a new beginning, a fresh start. So it is with your own story. You may be dried up right now, but that doesn't have to be your final destination. Along this journey, there is grace to be grasped, hope to be held, peace to be found, and promises to be mined.

Flourishing in Jesus is about leaving behind a shallow faith for a deeper walk with him. He isn't just a part of who you are; he *is* your life (see Colossians 3:4). Pursuing Jesus isn't about attaining perfection or arriving at a specific destination. It's not about having your life put together or avoiding suffering and struggles. It's about finding unending hope, peace, and strength in Jesus so you can conquer the challenges you face and flourish right where you've been planted. As a Well-Watered Woman, you won't have a perfect life, but it will be full of hope, brimming with purpose, and fueled by grace.

Because of Christ, your story has been rewritten, redefined, and redeemed. Your ultimate goal is a well-watered, abundant, and overflowing life. So don't waste your time dwelling on how shriveled up your faith has become. Instead, drink deeply from the Well and embrace the glory of a fresh start.

PART ONE

THE WELL

Whoever drinks of the water that I will give him shall never thirst;

but the water that I will give him will become in him

a well of water springing up to eternal life.

JOHN 4:13-14, NASB (EMPHASIS ADDED)

JESUS, THE WELL, fills the empty void in our souls. He meets us right where we are—in sin, shame, and suffering—and offers us salvation.

The Well represents the moment you meet Jesus and surrender your life to him. You coming to the Well isn't a one-time event. Our hearts become thirsty and parched every day, and only Jesus offers the kind of living water that always satisfies. No matter how empty your cup is, the Well is always brimming. The Well-Watered Woman pours herself out each day and returns to the Well over and over to meet with Jesus. No matter where she is on her journey, the Well is always available for refreshment and revival. Whether she finds herself in a season of plenty or a season of drought, she runs to the Well of living water for true soul satisfaction—and her very survival.

Your faith journey begins when the gospel seed is planted in your heart and takes root in the soil of your soul. When God plants the seed, he calls you to die to yourself in order to embrace new life in him. The deepening of your faith roots is a continual process of growing in the knowledge of who God is and how knowing him changes everything about your life.

Throughout Scripture, the well is a symbol of abundance, provision, and life. Just as wells provide for a practical need—water for the physically thirsty—they point to Christ, who supplies living water for the thirsty soul. When planted by God in the barren soul, the seed of the gospel satisfies and sustains the Well-Watered Woman through life's suffering, storms, and celebrations.

Meet Me at the Grace Well

Meet me at the Grace Well,
Where living waters flow,
To quench your thirsty heart
And satisfy your soul.

Come just as you are,
Broken, beaten, bruised.
Receive his endless love
And listen to Good News.

Bring your empty cup,
The one you've tried to fill
With treasures of this world,
Leaving you empty still.

It's not the water you know;
It's the water he freely gives.
It will revive your dead soul
So you can truly live.

Drink deeply from this Well
That never will run dry.
Hold tightly to his Word of truth,
Then worship with your life.

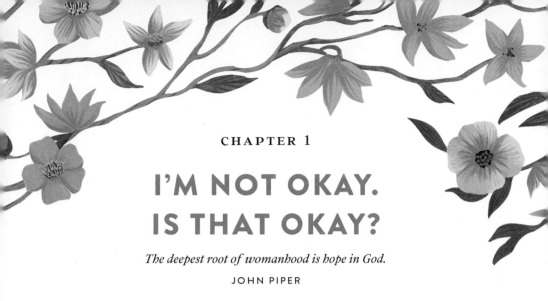

I'M NOT OKAY.
IS THAT OKAY?

The deepest root of womanhood is hope in God.

JOHN PIPER

The Story of a Thirsty Woman

She was a far cry from being "okay." For years, she tried to act as if she had it all together, putting on a smile as a Band-Aid against the hurt invading her soul. She ignored the brokenness that screamed for attention from deep within, and she became a pro at faking an "I'm fine" response to people's questions about how she was doing. Until . . . everything shattered. She could no longer wear a mask of perfection. She didn't even know how to put it on anymore. Her roots were shallow, and when the winds of change came, her tornado-like emotions blew her over. She finally admitted to herself and to the Lord, *I'm not okay.* But the question begged to be answered: *Is it okay for a Christian not to be okay?* She looked to Jesus and was surprised by the response.

AS I SAT IN THE OFFICE, I glanced around at the various plants growing in their respective clay pots. They looked no different from the week before, but still, they were alive and there was growth happening that was unseen by my human eye. These slow-growing plants felt like comrades to me. They reminded me of my own soul.

More often than not, I feel as if nothing is changing, as if I'm still stuck where I was last week and the week before that. But in reality, there's unseen change happening; there's growth beneath the surface. Through the hard questions and wrestlings of life, my roots are growing deeper. To be honest, I wish the growth was faster, more visible, more obvious. I wish I didn't need to sit in the office of a Christian counselor, seeking healing and understanding for my broken emotions and beliefs.

"How are you doing?" she asked.

Immediately the tears started to fall from my eyes. Her simple question opened a floodgate of turmoil that had been dammed up in my soul. The tears continued to flow as I unloaded the burdens, worries, and fears that overwhelmed my heart.

Ever since I had my first panic attack, it felt like my identity was in shambles. I lived each day as only a shadow of who I used to be. At the time, I didn't realize that through the undoing of my life, God was actually putting me back together again. Every tear that fell reflected not only my brokenness but also God's inner healing.

It's as if the tears were my soul's way of watering what God was doing inside of me. Without the rain falling, there can be no deepening of the roots, no growth for the plant. Without the tears falling, there can be no deepening of our faith, no growth in Christ. Tears can be a downpour that God uses to grow, nourish, and heal us from the inside out.

"I'm not doing okay," I confessed through embarrassed sobs. "And that's *not* okay."

"Isn't it?" she asked. "You know, it's okay for a Christian to not be okay."

Those words were hard for me to believe. Is it really okay to not be okay? I'd never heard this before, but for the first time, I felt the freedom to breathe. I'd spent most of my life striving after perfection, trying to be okay all the time, while the whole time I was sinking. This was turning out to be a suffocating pursuit.

As tears flooded my eyes, I recognized that it wasn't just that day I wasn't okay. I actually hadn't been okay for several years. I'd tried to cover up the gaping wounds of my soul, hoping it would make the bleeding stop, when I needed deeper healing that would mend the underlying root of my wound.

I was overcommitted, overwhelmed, overstimulated, and overtired—and I was over it. I knew something needed to change, but I didn't know where to go from there. The shallow roots of my heart had been plucked up by the storms of life, and I felt like I was being thrown around by gale-force winds. In the root system of my beliefs, I didn't think it was okay to not be okay, and I was falling apart.

HOW ARE YOU—*REALLY*?

If someone were to ask you how you're doing, what would you say? I have a hunch most of us default to something like "Good" or "Fine" or maybe even "Good but tired." We're breathing; we're alive. Therefore, we must be "good." Yet if you're like me, you're also a tad (okay, a lot) overwhelmed, you have a long to-do list to tackle, and you're physically, emotionally, and spiritually weary.

"Good" or "fine" is often what we say when we don't want to let someone in to see what's *really* going on inside. We're trying to move the conversation on to the next thing while ignoring the fact that we're being tossed around by the circumstances of our lives. The truth is, we live most of our days in between where "fine" meets exhausted, rushed, tired, and at the end of ourselves.

So how are you right now—*really*? Are you being tossed around by the stress of never-ending to-do lists? By despair and hopelessness? By self-pity and comparison? By the pressure to do better and achieve more? By piles of dirty dishes that seem to yell, "You are not in control!"? By the pursuit of success—trying hard but never arriving? By the reality of what it means to hold on to hope in a world that often feels hopeless?

If we have rooted ourselves in the shallow soil of this world—in what we do and what we can accomplish in life— we will struggle to survive the storms. Only when we're rooted in Christ can we experience a life that is real, secure, and free.

THE TALE OF A BLACK THUMB

I have to admit that I feel a little bit like a phony writing this book when I've got a track record of being a plant killer. The number of succulents and "easy to maintain" houseplants that have faced their last moments in my home is embarrassingly large. Nevertheless, I always learn lessons from these little plants, especially the ones that have the tenacity to survive.

When my husband, Greg, and I lived in the hills of Tennessee, a local plant nursery was right down the street from our home. I'd stop by occasionally to grab a new plant (or two) to replace the ones I'd killed. Around this time, a friend gave me a packet of zinnia seeds. The illustration on the front of the package depicted purple, fuchsia, and burnt-orange flowers with a tiny butterfly fluttering from one petal to the next. Each time I picked up the seed packet and admired the beautiful illustration, I would set the package back down, afraid to bury these beauties beneath the earth.

How could such a delightful plant grow from such a small seed? I marveled. The following spring, with the help of my father-in-law's green thumb, I nervously planted the seeds in a small plastic starter tray. Each morning I'd check on them, waiting for a speck of green to appear in the dark soil.

Eventually something caught my eye. Was it really a sign of *new* life? Sure enough, a small green sprout was shooting up from the depths.

After that, more and more sprouts began to appear in the

tray. As the days progressed, these small sprouts grew and grew until . . . I killed them. I went out of town and was unable to water my seedlings, and by the time I returned home, these little beauties had bitten the dust. (You didn't think my black thumb turned green that quickly, did you?)

This illustration depicts the well-watered life: imperfect and always in progress. The Well-Watered Woman isn't a perfect woman, but she knows the one who is perfect—the Gardener who never fails. She isn't always "okay" and she isn't always "fine," but she roots herself in the unrelenting hope of the gospel.

Sometimes she gets busy and distracted. Sometimes she neglects Bible study. Sometimes she sinks into the despair of this broken world. The difference is she doesn't stay in the "I'm not okay" moments forever. She always comes back to Christ, the cornerstone and foundation of her life. Here's the wisdom she's rooted in:

She knows God will not leave her side—ever (see Hebrews 13:5).
She knows she isn't enough apart from him, but in him, she has all she needs (see Ephesians 1:3).
She knows discouragement, failure, and doubt don't get the last word (see 2 Timothy 1:7; James 1:5-8).
She knows that it's okay to not be okay in this fallen world, because, in the end, all will be better than okay in Christ (see 2 Corinthians 4:8-12).

She knows feelings aren't something to be afraid of;
>
> she listens to them, learns from them, and leans on her
> Savior in the midst of them (see Psalm 42:1-3; 63:1-3).

The Well-Watered Woman is like a seed planted by God—continually growing by his grace, sustained by his promises.

THINGS WERE NOT OKAY IN THE BEGINNING

In the very beginning, before all that is was not yet, the earth is described as being "without form and void, and darkness was over the face of the deep" (Genesis 1:2). The earth was not okay when it first began. The Hebrew word for "formlessness" is *tohu*.[1] There was no order, no life, and no light, but the Creator God brought life, light, beauty, and purpose from its vast, empty surface. From nothing, God created everything. From a wasteland, he made wonder.

God knew what he was doing when he created light, land, and water before creating vegetation and plants (see Genesis 1:3-5). The great Gardener created the perfect conditions for growth at the dawn of time. Today he shows his creativity, power, and provision as he cultivates the conditions for new life to grow within our souls. He is infinitely patient, and he takes the long view when it comes to our growth.

When I planted those tiny seeds in the starter trays, some were almost too small to see. Multiple seedlings fell into one hole to offer an opportunity for one or two to take root. After planting, I showered them with some water, set them by a window, and began the hard part: waiting.

Did you know you can't make a plant grow faster by staring at it? It's true; I tried. What I was forgetting was that growth was happening beneath the soil long before the green sprouts were visible. Each day I watered and waited, and all the while, God worked.

YOU ARE NOT OKAY WITHOUT JESUS

The creation story beautifully reflects the salvation story. God, the Author of life and Creator of time, brings new life to struggling, chaotic, not-okay human souls. God isn't just the one who created our bodies; he also creates the conditions for our spiritual growth.

The apostle Paul used this analogy in his letter to the church at Corinth: "I planted, Apollos watered, but God gave the growth. So neither he who plants nor he who waters is anything, but only God who gives the growth" (1 Corinthians 3:6-7). Though we do our part to dig holes, drop seeds, cover them with soil, and water them, growth and life ultimately come from God. Just as God made the soil and designed the seeds to produce food and beauty for life, he created the spiritual conditions for us to know him and follow him. Just as he set the sun on fire and caused the earth to spin at perfect speed—not too fast, not too slow—he set our hearts to long for him and for eternity (see Ecclesiastes 3:11).

God placed the first human beings in a perfect, beautiful garden. But this idyllic scene didn't last long, and from the moment they ate the forbidden fruit, Adam and Eve weren't okay (see Genesis 3). The earth wasn't okay either. It was cursed, broken, and ravaged by sin, and we still reap those effects today. After Adam and Eve's rebellion, God spoke directly to them, sharing the consequences for their disobedience. To Adam, he said, "Cursed is the ground because of you; in pain you shall eat of it all the days of your life; thorns and thistles it shall bring forth for you; and you shall eat the plants of the field" (Genesis 3:17-18). The earth that was made to bear fruit would now also bear thorns and thistles, pain and disappointment, suffering and sorrow. In your struggle with jealousy, thorns grow. In your bitterness against the person who betrayed you, thorns grow. In your desire for something God hasn't given you, thorns grow.

The thorns that came into the earth because of the Curse were just the beginning. Later, those thorns inflicted pain that has never been felt before and will never be felt again: at the crucifixion of Christ. The pain Jesus endured on the cross was more than physical torture. He also endured the wrath of God against sin and shouldered the weight of human depravity (see Isaiah 53:10). The very Curse Adam had reaped due to his disobedience was set on Jesus' head in the form of a crown of thorns (see Romans 5:12-21; Galatians 3:13).

Christ became "not okay" for us so we could be more than

okay forever in him (see Romans 5:8). Christ, the one who created the lush, green world and brought life and wonder from nothing, reaped the consequences of sin *for* us. It's almost too scandalous to be true. That's why the gospel both wrecks us and restores us. It's so wonderful, so indescribable, so layered with grace that it takes an entire lifetime and all of eternity for us to truly grasp it. Christ redeemed the thorns of this life by wearing them for us (see Matthew 27:29). Now we're no longer bound by crushing circumstances or stuck in unrelenting strongholds; we are free, and we are finally okay—more than okay—in him.

Even in the moments when life is not okay—when the sheriff shows up at the front door with tragic news, when the e-mail pops up with a shocking story, when your child rebels and leaves your home—remember the crown of thorns piercing the perfect brow of Christ, who is now risen and wearing an eternal crown of glory (see Revelation 19:12). The Well-Watered Woman is not the perfect woman, but she knows the perfect one who was pierced with thorns in her place. The thorns of suffering and sorrow may still grow, but they don't pierce us forever. Any pain we feel is meant to point us back to Christ, who wore the crown of thorns to break the curse caused by sin.

Charles Spurgeon, known as the "prince of preachers," said, "Thorns and thistles shall the earth bring forth to thee, but if these bring thee nearer to thy God, they are the best crop the ground can grow!"[2]

YOU ARE MORE THAN OKAY IN CHRIST

If you were to ask me how I'm doing now that I've finished writing this chapter, I would respond differently. While I still have a long to-do list in front of me, a house in disarray around me, and a lot of emotions stirring inside me, the Word of truth is at work, refocusing me and reminding me that God is good, even now. My circumstances haven't changed, but the posture of my heart shifts as I look to Jesus (see Hebrews 12:1-3). Though I still have things that concern me, I'm reminded of God's care. This is what God's Word does to our feelings and our present struggles—it gives us what we need, right when we need it (see Philippians 4:19).

When your roots run deep in God's goodness and steadfast love, nothing can shake you or break you forever. His goodness and unfailing love hold us together when life is falling apart. They provide a healing balm when thorns strike our souls. When we're not okay, we remember that our attitudes of praise are dependent not on the ease of our circumstances but on the fact that God is good—period (see Psalm 136). This is why the apostle Paul prayed for believers who were walking through suffering—that they not lose heart but become "rooted and grounded in love" and that they "know the love of Christ that surpasses knowledge" (Ephesians 3:13-19). You can never be empty when you're full of Jesus.

The very one who made and redeemed the world will also one day restore the world to be *better* than okay—it will be glorious and even better than Eden.[3] The thorns of suffering, sorrow, doubt, and discouragement will no longer grow or take root in our hearts (see Revelation 21:1-5). Instead, we will harvest life, joy, abundance, and peace as we dwell forever with God, whose very presence will give us light (see Revelation 22:5). Until that glorious day, we wait as God tends the soil of our hearts (see Romans 8:19-25).

In this in-between time, we embrace the realities of living in a fallen world while being deeply rooted in the infallible Word of God. These roots cannot be plucked up or pulled out of the soil. They are steadfast and immovable, and they grow deeper and deeper day by day. In the moments when things are not okay, those roots keep us grounded in the truth we already know.

Hold fast to the Word of God, and it will hold fast to you. Living a well-watered life doesn't mean always being okay. It does mean you're always growing more attached to Jesus and less attached to this world. Even in the daily, unseen moments, the Gardener is tending your soul and making you whole.

So wait with hope. One day, everything will be better than okay in him. Until then, let the thorns and thistles of life thrust you closer to him and pierce your heart with gospel truth.

THE WELL-WATERED WOMAN

SURRENDERS A LIFE

OF STRIVING

FOR A LIFE

OF SINKING HER ROOTS

INTO GOD'S WORD.

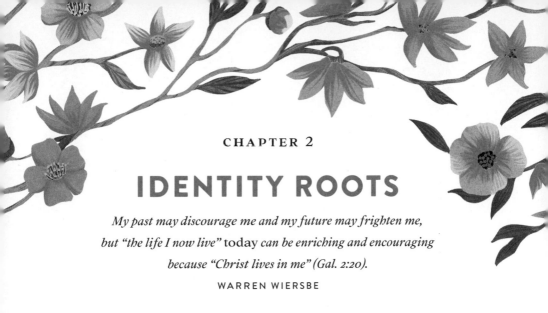

CHAPTER 2

IDENTITY ROOTS

*My past may discourage me and my future may frighten me,
but "the life I now live" today can be enriching and encouraging
because "Christ lives in me" (Gal. 2:20).*

WARREN WIERSBE

The Story of a Thirsty Woman

Gazing in the mirror, she studied the stranger squinting back at her. *Who am I?* she wondered. Along the way, she'd lost her identity amid the expectations that had been placed on her—by others and by herself. Comparison stole her confidence, and insecurity stripped her peace. Her past haunted her, and her future terrified her. She didn't know who she was, and she wandered aimlessly, trying to find her true identity. She was lost in the myriad of lies she had come to accept as true. Would she ever be able to pull up the rotten roots buried deep in her heart? Would she ever know who she really was . . . and who she was meant to be?

STORM CLOUDS SWIRLED in the sky as the salty ocean breeze wrapped around us in a misty hug. Waves crashed on the shore, reminding me how small and vulnerable I really am. Undaunted, my husband and I set off to explore the shoreline before the storm set in.

Sturdy ironwood trees lined the coast of the beach in Kauai, showing off impressive root systems that had been gradually exposed by harsh wind and high waves. The roots spread out like an enormous maze, becoming more intricate the deeper they had gone into the ground.

The root systems appeared to be larger than the trees themselves. As I stood on the sand with the roots towering over me, my five-foot-ten-inch frame seemed comparably short. I grabbed hold of one of the thick roots and began to swing like a free-spirited child. The root didn't even budge with my added weight. It turned out that the constant blowing of the wind and the crashing of the waves hadn't just exposed the roots; the elements had made them stronger.

The waves of life crash over us, too. They expose our roots—where our identity really stems from. Our core beliefs—whether true or false—become stronger and more fortified through the storms of life. We often don't know what we truly believe about God and ourselves until trials, testing, and temptation crash over us, exposing what is beneath the surface. If our roots are strong and grounded in a bedrock of truth, we'll remain steady and grow stronger for the next storm. If not, we'll be tossed around and ultimately knocked down.

THE ROOTS WE NEVER WANTED

After a seed is buried beneath the earth's surface, its first priority is to develop roots in the soil. Roots are the heartbeat of the plant—they absorb nutrients in the soil, take in water, and stabilize the plant. Without roots, plants can't grow, flourish, or produce fruit. Without their invisible work beneath the surface, there would be no life above. The strongest trees and toughest plants are the ones with the deepest roots . . . and often the ones that have faced the most storms.

One of my simple joys in life is store-bought flower bouquets in the dead of winter. They bring life and beauty to our home—a reminder in even the harshest of conditions that good things still grow. But they last only a short time because they've been cut off from their life source. The moment these beauties are cut, the clock begins ticking until their inevitable withering and eventual death. Unlike perennials, plants that come back to life year after year, these flowers can provide only temporary satisfaction. What makes the difference? The roots.

Your identity has roots—unseen, hidden, yet manifested in how you live. Our sense of identity is ultimately rooted in what we believe about God and ourselves. When these beliefs aren't rooted in the truth, chaos ensues. Maybe your identity is rooted in past experiences, perceived failures, or false words that were spoken over you. Or perhaps your identity is rooted in a present situation that's making you feel stuck and disappointed. Your identity could be rooted in future fears, potential mistakes, or a sense of upcoming doom. Most likely, your roots are tangled up in all three—past pain, present struggles, and future worries. I know this has been true for me.

Although I grew up in a Christian home and have been a follower of Christ for most of my life, many of my core beliefs have stood in stark contrast to God's truth. Tracing these roots, I went all the way back to my childhood, when I began to believe Satan's lies over God's truth.

As early as kindergarten, I remember the sting of being left out and feeling different from others. I thought that people didn't like me for who I was and that in order to be liked, I had to earn their affections. One of the girls I desperately wanted to be friends with invited me to her birthday party, and I was thrilled. But not long after I got there, I ate a hot dog and got sick. It wasn't a pretty sight, and I wasn't invited to play with that group of girls again. This experience deepened the lie that I was flawed beyond repair.

Rotten root: What others think of you is more important than what God thinks of you.

Gospel root: When God sees you, he sees Christ, not your past failures or mistakes. Your worth is determined by who created you—the God of heaven and earth. The only audience to live for is the audience of one.

When I was in third grade, our family moved from El Paso, Texas, to Atlanta, Georgia, which was a culture shock, to say the least. I'd never seen tall trees or skyscrapers before, and I was excited about this new adventure. But at my new school, I still didn't fit in. A boy who lived in our apartment complex spread rumors about me, and once again, I felt like an outcast. Already in those early years, I learned how to mask my struggles and put on a happy face, even when I was hurting. This practice followed me into my adult years.

Rotten root: You have to mask your hurt with a happy face.

Gospel root: Christ has experienced the hurt for you. He understands, he listens, he is with you, and he can handle your hurting heart. Bring the pain to him, and receive his promise of healing (see Isaiah 53:5).

When I was a young adult, I believed I had to be a certain size and have a certain body type to be beautiful and loved. I wouldn't put on a bathing suit unless I'd done sit-ups or exercised. I constantly compared myself to every woman around me, and I was drowning in defeat.

Rotten root: True beauty is determined by your weight, skin color, and size.

Gospel root: Your worth is determined by your Savior, who bore the weight of the world on his shoulders to set you free (see John 8:32).

When I was a young mama, I believed my value came from what I accomplished—from how well behaved my kids were or whether they made me look good—and what I checked off my to-do list each day.

Rotten root: In order to be successful and have worth, you must be constantly productive and never take a break.

Gospel root: You can never do enough or be enough to satisfy the masses. The most productive thing you can do is to love God with all your heart, soul, mind, and strength, and to love your neighbor as yourself (see Matthew 22:37-38).

If we believe Satan's lies, we'll find our lives drained of joy, and we'll lose our ability to delight in God's goodness and grace. Satan wants to keep us stuck in these lies, many of which stem from our beginnings, in an attempt to win the battle for our identities. This is why Satan will do everything possible to keep you from opening your Bible. He knows his lies can't stand against the truth of God's Word.

The more I began to hunger for God's Word, the more the Holy Spirit exposed the lies I believed about God and myself. I began the necessary cutting away of these deeply rooted lies so I could experience freedom from everything that wasn't true and so I could truly believe God's Word.

IDENTITY ROOTS BEGIN AT BIRTH

From the moment you were born, your identity roots began to form. Early childhood experience creates the groundwork for your belief system—for better or worse. Even the happiest of children grow up with incorrect core beliefs about who God is, as well as who they are or who they believe they should be. These beliefs are like tree roots that dig down deep over time. As the tree grows upward, the roots continue to grow down-ward. Good roots produce good fruit; rotten roots produce rotten fruit—or no fruit at all.

What we believe about who God is and who we are in him will be exposed when the wind and waves of life buffet our souls. Though we try to hide the brokenness of our past, the instability of our present, or the uncertainty of our future, we will eventually be exposed. As Jesus explained to his disciples, "Out of the abundance of the heart the mouth speaks. The good person out of his good treasure brings forth good, and the evil person out of his evil treasure brings forth evil" (Matthew 12:34-35).

I often don't know what I really think or believe until I start writing or talking. In the outpouring of words, my spiritual eyes can see what's really growing in my soul. And most of the time, it's not the prettiest picture. When my husband gives me a compliment, my first response is to balk at it and retort the opposite. Why? Because deep in my soul, I don't believe his words to be true. I'm convinced I am broken and unworthy of love. I've forgotten my true identity in Christ—that in him, I'm a new creation, deeply loved, and made on purpose (see 2 Corinthians 5:17; Ephesians 2:10; 1 John 3:1). In him, I am loved, cherished, and seen (see 1 Samuel 16:7; Psalm 33:13; 1 Peter 2:9-10). In him, I am free (see John 8:32; Galatians 5:1). Even if our initial response is toxic, we can choose to pluck out the rotting roots and tend the good roots instead. Through the plucking and the tending, we'll be able to live in our identity as children of God.

Earlier this year, when my doctor told me I needed a biopsy of a potentially cancerous nodule on my thyroid gland, I found myself questioning God, playing my tiny violin in a concert of self-pity. Instead of praying and trusting God, the first thing I did was send a text to my husband, my mom, and my sister, complaining that God just never lets me have a break.

"*Why* me? *Why* this? *Why* now?" I asked over and over.

This exposed a lie in my core that, as a Christian, I shouldn't have to suffer or be needy. I wanted to be the helper, not the helped. I wanted to be healthy, not in need of medicine. But Scripture says just the opposite: "'My grace is sufficient for you, for my power is made perfect in weakness.' Therefore I will boast all the more gladly of my weaknesses, so that the power of Christ may rest upon me" (2 Corinthians 12:9). God never promised me a pain-free life—in fact, the challenges are the places where he reveals his glory best.

Another false identity root pulled up.

Though the test came back with no sign of cancer, I'm still not in the clear—and I never will be this side of heaven. Through that unexpected hurdle, I learned that even if the biopsy had come back revealing a cancer diagnosis, God would still be good, whether or not this is my first response. It seems that once I'm on the other side of one trial, it's on to the next one. And it doesn't have to be the big things—the daily details of life have the potential to derail me too.

When my plans for a perfect family trip go down the drain, I often lose sight of the beauty happening in the brokenness. My complaining drowns out the blessings that are constantly flowing down. Not long ago, my husband and I planned a day out with our boys at the aquarium in Atlanta. Apparently, the rest of Atlanta had the same idea, because the place was jam-packed. Our boys wanted to be held the whole time, and we could barely see the fish darting around in their tanks. Our day was thrown off-kilter from the start, and it was nothing like the Instagram-worthy outing I had in mind.

I've lived most of my life in the shadow of discouragement as my unrealistic expectations unravel. *Why?* Because I believe life should be perfect, and if reality doesn't live up to my standard of perfection, it must be a waste of time and effort. I place my hope in earthly perfection, which God has never promised me, instead of in my Savior, who promises redemption and beauty out of broken places, plans, and people.

Our core beliefs shape our thoughts, which embody our actions. If you want to know what you truly believe, take note of the thoughts that tumble through your mind. What do you dream about? What discourages you or unsettles you? What sets your soul on fire?

Not only do our core beliefs shape our thoughts; they are also the source of our words and actions. At the end of each day, survey your responses and decisions, and trace them all the way down to the root. What underlying belief produced the action? What belief about yourself or God led to those words? What kind of fruit is that belief producing? If it's rotten fruit, how can this belief be exposed and cut away with the hacksaw of truth?

You won't be able to remove a rotten identity root in one day. But when you make it a practice to take your thoughts captive and make them obedient to Christ and his Word (see 2 Corinthians 10:5), your beliefs will gradually shift, and new roots will be created.

THE SOIL OF YOUR SOUL

The ironwood tree, indigenous to Australia, was first intro-duced to the shores of Hawaii in 1895.[1] This tree is known for its ability to take root in even the poorest of soils, which explains why it can survive along a pounding ocean shore. Just as the ironwood tree can put its roots in sand or good soil, identity can take root in both lies and truth. The good and the bad can mingle together in the foundation of who you are as a person—and this foundation affects who you are at this very moment.

I have learned firsthand that even if your roots are bad, hope is not lost. God can restore even the most poisonous belief sys-tem with healthy roots. The gospel uproots the lies buried in our souls and plants truth in their place. This isn't a one-time event, of course. It involves daily renewal as God allows the waves of life to wash over our souls, exposing what should stay and what should go.

The waves aren't always a welcome gift, though. When waves come and crash against my soul, the first thing I want to do is shield myself from the blows. Charles Spurgeon report-edly said, "I have *learned* to kiss the waves that throw me up against the Rock of Ages" (emphasis added). In other words, he recognized that waves will always come; it's how we respond to the waves that makes all the difference. The learned response of embracing these waves as gifts of grace comes when we consider how Christ embraced the tsunami of sin on the cross.

Though Jesus wrestled to the point that drops of blood poured from his brow, he kissed the wave and prayed, "Not my will, but yours, be done" (Luke 22:42-44).

This is exactly what the ironwood trees on the shores of Kauai do each day—they kiss the waves. Their exposed roots make them stronger, not to mention breathtaking. Which brings me to a question I grapple with, one that both haunts me and frees my soul: *Could it be that the waves of life actually produce in us a deeper, stronger, more tenacious identity in Christ that wouldn't exist without the raging storms and pounding surf?*

Scripture reveals this mystery of growth from Genesis to Revelation. Every person mentioned in the Bible faced hardship. Some had identity crises. Some survived and flourished in the wake of trials, while others were killed for their faith. But not everyone learned to kiss the waves. The ones who did came to know God more deeply. Many of these people are listed in Hebrews 11, often known as the "hall of faith." The writer of Hebrews describes them this way: "These all died in faith, not having received the things promised, but having seen them and greeted them from afar, and having acknowledged that they were strangers and exiles on the earth." They desired "a better country, that is, a heavenly one" (Hebrews 11:13, 16).

God can use our trials to show the world that his grace is greater. He can transform the waves that crash onto our shore into gifts that sever rotten roots and strengthen our true identity in him. The identity roots of those listed in the hall of faith weren't in their present or their past but in the unchanging, unwavering, always-loving God . . . and their secure future with him. The same offer is available to us, as well.

GOOD ROOTS PRODUCE GOOD FRUIT

When I first started gardening, I was what you might call overly ambitious. Instead of planting just one tomato plant, I planted ten. Since we were living in a rental home and couldn't have a traditional garden, I put each plant in its own pot. Some hung by hooks on the porch, and others were scattered around the yard. A few weeks into tending these tomato plants, I noticed that one of them wasn't growing like the others. The leaves were turning yellow, and the sprouts were dying off. I'd been caring for each plant the same way, but this one wasn't producing the way it should. I finally decided to repot the pesky plant so I could try to identify the problem.

When I tipped over the pot, I was overcome by a pungent odor. Below the surface of the plant, down in the soil, the roots were rotting. In my rookie gardening knowledge, I'd failed to open the bottom of the plastic pot, leaving no drainage system. All the water I'd given the plant sat at the bottom of the container with no place to go. The plant grew for a short time until the problems under the surface became obvious in the plant above.

When your identity roots rot, your life will begin to reflect what is happening to the roots. It may be subtle at first, but you can't produce good, lasting fruit without good, healthy roots. God doesn't just care about the fruit of our lives; he first tends to our roots.

In order to survive and thrive, our souls need proper drainage systems. If we allow every thought or belief to sit in the bottom of our souls with no way to drain out, we'll quickly become like my rotting tomato plant—unfruitful and stunted in our growth. We need a way to get rid of the harmful thoughts that get lodged at our core. I call this "thought sifting." What we hear and believe must be sifted through the truth of God's Word.

Ultimately, what we believe about who God is and who we are in him affects the way we live and think, and these beliefs are buried in the root system of our souls. If we have good roots, our lives will produce the good fruit of the Spirit (see Galatians 5:22-23). These roots can be established and strengthened only when they're watered by the truth of Scripture and cleansed from the lies of this world.

When our identity roots are healthy, they don't affect just our own lives. Good roots create the foundation for good fruit for you, for others, and for the glory of God.

FIGHTING ROOT ROT IN THE GARDEN OF YOUR SOUL

Becoming a "thought sifter" happens only when we're able to distinguish a rotten thought from a good one, and this happens only through knowing God's Word. We'll never be free from the lies if we don't know the truth (see John 8:32). We'll never survive the storms if we don't root ourselves in good soil. We'll never live the well-watered life if we don't have a good drainage system to help our roots grow and our lives flourish. When the waves of life wash over us and the storm clouds form above, we need identity roots that are grounded in the gospel so we can "kiss the waves" and cling to Christ.

I lived most of my life with rotten roots forming the foundation of my actions, feelings, and thoughts. Though I was in church every Sunday (and Monday and Wednesday and probably more days than that), deep down I didn't truly believe that God is good, and that God is good to me. Every wave that crashed against the shore of my soul sent me tumbling downward, wondering whether God would set me free or fail me. My desire for perfection—for myself, others, and my circumstances—created rotting roots of despair, hopelessness, and discouragement.

When I was in high school, my dad unexpectedly lost his job, and somehow I felt responsible. I believed that God was punishing our family due to my lack of faith, so I started praying more, trying to convince God that we were good enough and he should provide for us. I bought into the lie that if I were faithful enough, we would receive a "get out of suffering" pass.

Over time, when things didn't seem to get better with my dad's work situation, I finally opened up to my mom. Through wrenching sobs, I told her I thought God wasn't being faithful to our family because my faith was lacking. On top of that, I wasn't tithing as much as I could have from my babysitting money. I'd misunderstood the central message of the gospel—that I'm hopeless and helpless apart from Christ but that his grace is sufficient (see 2 Corinthians 12:9). He is still faithful to us even when we are faithless (see 2 Timothy 2:13).

Over the next decade, the root rot began to stink, and the stench wasn't affecting only me; it was affecting my husband, my children, my family, my friends, and my ministry.

It finally hit me: the roots of my life, though often hidden from the human eye, eventually become evident through the aroma of my life and the fruit it produces (or doesn't produce). If I want to embrace the life Jesus died to make possible, I have to dig up the rotten roots with the shovel of God's Word and, with the Holy Spirit's help, plant truth. And this isn't a one-time event; the garden of my soul is always in need of care. Every day I must dig up and replace rotten roots with good, true thoughts.

When our roots begin to show, like the ironwood trees on the shore of Kauai, may they be a spectacle drawing people to the glory of God. Because strong roots don't form on their own. They become strong through the battering of the waves and the storms, and most important, the sustaining grace of God.

THE WELL-WATERED WOMAN

KNOWS WHO JESUS IS,

AND WHO HE IS

CHANGES EVERYTHING

ABOUT HER PAST, PRESENT,

AND FUTURE.

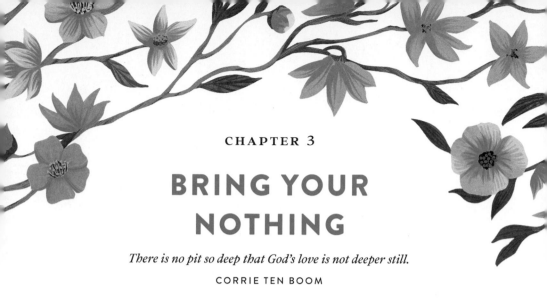

BRING YOUR NOTHING

There is no pit so deep that God's love is not deeper still.

CORRIE TEN BOOM

The Story of a Thirsty Woman

Her brokenness betrayed her. Just when she thought she'd hidden her faults, they tumbled out of the junk closet of her heart, plain for all to see. Years of hiding had imprisoned her in the shadows of despair. Darkness clouded her soul, and shame wreaked havoc in the depths of her being. The thing she feared most—exposure— was the only way to freedom, the only key to set her free from prison. Tired of being trapped in the bondage of sin and broken- ness, she needed to walk toward the light, baggage and all. If she brought her empty cup to Jesus, could he actually fill it up with his grace?

CROUCHING ON THE COLD LAMINATE FLOOR, I sobbed as I looked at the strands of hair laced around my fingers. Months of starving myself had finally taken a toll on my health, and the lack of nourishment caused my body to let go of anything unnecessary for survival. Hiding in the bathroom of my college apartment, I never wanted to be seen again. The full chestnut hair that once crowned my head had started to fall to the ground—a visible reminder of my sin and brokenness. *How could the promise of beauty cost me everything?* I wondered. Hot, salty tears rolled down my cheeks, pouring from a broken heart.

Just minutes before, my roommates had confronted me about my eating disorder. As I look back now, I can see that they were doing this out of love and compassion, but in the moment, it felt like a dagger directly to my heart.

I'd just returned to our apartment after an outing with friends when I found the girls I lived with huddled in the living room, waiting for me. "If you don't do something about this, we're going to take you to the hospital," one said.

I couldn't say anything in response—I simply stood there, trembling and completely undone. What I thought I had hidden was obvious to everyone.

Not knowing what to do, I went upstairs and called my mom, desperate for help. As I sat in my room alone, waiting for my mom to make the hour-long drive to my apartment, I felt like a complete failure. It was as if my sin had been plastered on a movie screen for everyone to see and judge, and I didn't think I would ever recover from the shame and embarrassment. Despair descended on my soul like a mighty cloud, and all I wanted to do was hide from the storm swirling in my heart. That day I built a wall of protection around myself—a wall to keep people from seeing how broken and bruised I really was.

There was only one way for that wall to come down: the wrecking ball of the gospel.

GROWING UP A GOOD GIRL

Twelve years before my bathroom-floor breaking point, I walked down an aisle at the church my dad pastored in El Paso, Texas, to surrender my life to Jesus. I remember it like it was yesterday. Each week my parents would load me and my siblings in the family van and drive us along desert roads to the church, which was hemmed in by white sand and tall, gangly cacti. Dad would stand at the pulpit each Sunday and preach a message I typically didn't pay much attention to because I was too busy coloring or daydreaming in the wooden front pew.

That day was different, though. The ears of my heart tuned in to a message I hadn't understood before: the gospel of Jesus Christ. My heart pounded in my chest as I grasped for the first time that I was a sinner in need of a Savior. Standing in my Sunday dress, I took a step forward during the altar call to talk to my dad. After we got home, he and my mom walked me through the gospel message and what it means to be a follower of Jesus, and then they prayed with me. The next Sunday I put on a white robe and was immersed in a baptistery at the front of the church, an outward expression of my status as a new creation in Christ.

I'll admit, those early days after my salvation weren't much different from the ones before. I went on my way attempting to live the "good girl" life. By the time I reached middle school, I knew how to talk the Christian talk and walk the Christian walk. At the Christian high school I attended, the staff gave out a "Best Christian" award each year, and I was the recipient several times. The standard of being the "best" became an unreachable expectation I placed on myself, and I had the trophies on my bookshelf to remind me of it.

As well-meaning as the award was, it skewed my understanding of grace and the gospel for many years, and I added it to my "good girl" résumé. Though I loved Jesus, it was years before that love turned into a deeper understanding of the weight and glory of the gospel. As an aspiring good girl, I was a rule follower and a people pleaser. I sought affirmation through achievement and tried to avoid punishment at all costs. My longing for perfection kept me in a cycle of shame and disappointment. When I was performing well, I felt good about myself, but when I messed up, my first thought was to run away and hide. In a way, hiding became my specialty.

GOING FROM GOLD TO LAST PLACE

Daydreamer that I was, I frequently pretended to be someone else: a princess, a ballerina, an artist, a teacher, a maid, a trash collector (yes, you read that right!), or a waitress. My first memory of trying to escape my own failure happened not long after I gave my life to Jesus.

On this particular day, I decided to pretend I was a gymnast. Mom was running errands, and I was home with my older brother and sister. The living room of our quaint baby-blue home had a tweed couch with a sturdy back on it. Eyeing the frame of the couch, I saw the perfect balance beam where I could practice for my future as an Olympic gymnast. The US gymnastics team's victory was still fresh in my mind, and I'd decided I wanted to be an Olympic athlete too.

Taking my stand on the "balance beam," I held out my arms horizontally and navigated my way across, dipping one foot to the left and one to the right. Every other step, I'd add a tiny little hop to my performance as the imaginary crowd cheered wildly. Nearing the end of my routine, I prepared for the grand finale that would win me gold on that hot Texas day.

As I began my descent, my foot knocked the lamp off the side table, sending it crashing to the floor. The crowd fell silent. Hopping off the couch, I jetted to my room, shut the door, and hid under my bed, hoping the lamp would magically fix itself before my parents noticed it was broken. Unfortunately, that wasn't the last time I hid. And the stakes only grew higher in terms of what I had the potential to break.

A HISTORY OF HIDING

Hiding from sin isn't anything new. As a matter of fact, it goes all the way back to the very beginning, when Adam and Eve sinned and hid from God. After God created the heavens and the earth and everything in it, he finished off his masterpiece with the grand finale: humankind. God created man and woman as his image bearers to tend to the Garden and enjoy unbroken fellowship with him (see Genesis 1:26-27).

The Creation account gives us an important detail about the first man and woman: they were naked and not ashamed (see Genesis 2:25). There was no need for clothing because there was no need to cover anything up. It wasn't until Genesis 3 that sin entered the world, bringing with it shame. After Adam and Eve rebelled against God and ate the forbidden fruit, their eyes were opened to the nakedness of their bodies and souls (see Genesis 3:6-7). Their first inclination was to cover up God's once-perfect creation and hide.

Their feeble attempt to hide was in vain, however. God summoned Adam and Eve from the darkness of hiding and exposed their fear—not for the purpose of shaming them but to draw them to surrender and freedom. He didn't leave them in their hiding place, and he doesn't leave us in hiding either. From the very beginning, God has been calling his people out of hiding to live in the light of his grace. Our struggles and our strongholds go all the way back to the Garden . . . but so does our *hope*.

After God called Adam and Eve out from their hiding place, he cursed the serpent and proclaimed the first gospel message: that a Savior would come to crush the enemy (see Genesis 3:15). God brought a promise of hope in response to the first low moment of human history. As the narrative of Scripture unfolds, it reveals God's plan of redemption—all of which points us to Jesus. Redemption is what calls us out of our hiding places—not just once but as an ongoing pursuit.

Thousands of years later, the Son of God, who had been foretold in Genesis 3:15, was born. When Jesus came, he flipped the world upside down and, in doing so, turned it right side up again (see Matthew 1:23; Romans 5:6). He sat with sinners, preached to Pharisees, loved the lowly, touched the tainted, and healed the hurting. He came full of grace and truth—grace to conquer the ravaging effects of sin and shame, and truth to trump the lies of the enemy (see John 1:17).

But what does all this mean for us today? What does it mean for a girl hiding under the bed, afraid of getting in trouble? For a teen crouching on the floor weeping, consumed by an eating disorder? For a woman whose past convinces her she's broken beyond repair? For a mom who feels like no one sees the things she does behind the scenes?

The story of redemption means everything! It's every bit as

meaningful to us today as it was to the first people who tried to hide in their brokenness. Christ came to save the hopeless, scarred, and tainted. By his shed blood, he removes our sin and shame and gives us new names and new identities. As Isaiah 53:5 says, "With his wounds we are healed." This gospel message isn't just an invitation for the day we're saved; it's what we need preached to our hearts every moment of our lives.

THE GRACE WELL

There's a woman in the New Testament whose name isn't shared but whose story has been told for centuries. She's known as the woman at the well, but I like to think of her as a dried-up woman who became a Well-Watered Woman after encountering Jesus at "the Grace Well." She was searching for satisfaction in the wrong places, only to be left hopeless, alone, and still searching. She's just like you and me: needy, broken, hiding, and in need of rescuing. And here's the amazing part: Jesus met her in her ordinary, mundane life and changed the course of her future.

In John 4, we get to be spectators of this rather unusual event. Jesus, a Jewish man, met a woman from Samaria at a well in the heat of the day. In that era, it would have been unheard of for a respectable Jewish man to converse with a woman from Samaria with a disgraceful past. But Jesus came with a wrecking ball of gospel truth, shattering cultural barriers to display the Kingdom of God in everyday life. The apostle John describes Jesus as being "wearied" from his journey, but he "*had* to pass through Samaria" (John 4:4, 6, emphasis added). In other words, Jesus' meeting with this unnamed woman was no accident; it was a divine appointment.

"Give me a drink," Jesus said to her (John 4:7). She responded the way we often do—with excuses and her own unworthiness. With veiled eyes, she talked to the long-awaited Messiah, and she almost missed him. Sometimes I wonder how many moments we miss with Jesus because we're so distracted by our own shortcomings. We doubt Jesus would meet with us in the first place. But even though this woman wasn't looking for him, he found her—right in her place of need.

Jesus told her, "If you knew the gift of God, and who it is that is saying to you, 'Give me a drink,' you would have asked him, and he would have given you living water" (John 4:10). *Living Water.* Water that breathes life into the lifeless body. Water that refreshes the soul forever. Water that has the power to save. The Living Water Jesus offered this woman at the grace well was foreign to her hurting soul. It was exactly what she didn't know she needed but had spent her whole life searching for— the quenching kind of hope, love, and peace that can only be found in him.

NO WELL IS TOO DEEP

The woman responds to Jesus' invitation with a profound yet practical problem: "Sir, you have nothing to draw water with, and the well is deep. Where do you get that living water?" (John 4:11). *The well is deep.* Think about that for a moment. Don't we say this same thing to Jesus?

> *Jesus, my past is too stained and messy for you to redeem.*
> *If you knew what I've struggled with, you would have already*
>   *given up on me.*
> *My present is full of problems that are too big for you to handle.*
> *I am full of fear and worry over the unknowns of the future.*

We come to Jesus with our excuses and our assumptions that he can't redeem our brokenness. But Jesus knows the truth.

> No well is too deep for him.
> No past is too broken for him.
> No present is too out of reach for him.
> No future is too unpredictable for him.
> No wall is too high for him.
> No stronghold is too strong for him.

This is the Good News of the gospel—that he meets us in our brokenness and redeems us! This is what transforms a dried-up life into a well-watered life. This is what Jesus came to give the woman at the well, and it's what he came to give us, too.

Jesus said, "Everyone who drinks of this water will be thirsty again, but whoever drinks of the water that I will give him will never be thirsty again. The water that I will give him will become in him a spring of water welling up to eternal life" (John 4:13-14). What the world offers is temporary, but what Jesus offers is eternal. We can patch over our brokenness with worldly anecdotes, sayings, and quick fixes, but ultimately, it's the gospel message that redeems, revives, and restores.

What happens next in the story makes my jaw drop. Jesus called this woman out of hiding. When he told her to summon her husband, she said she had no husband. She had five previous husbands, and the man she was living with wasn't her husband (see John 4:16-18). Jesus, being fully God, knew all this, and he still talked to her. He knew all this, and he still called her. He knew all this, and he still offered her living water. Jesus offered her a drink that changed her for all eternity. She came with her guilt, and Christ met her with his grace.

BRING YOUR NOTHING; RECEIVE HIS EVERYTHING

The grace well never runs dry, and it doesn't come with stipulations. When Jesus called this woman to drink of the Living Water, he didn't give her a to-do list or tell her to get her act together first. No, he invited her to bring her nothing and receive his everything. He reached his hand into the muddy pit she was in and lifted her up. He brought her out of hiding and into the glorious light of grace and freedom. Her dried-up life was transformed into a well-watered life that day, and my hunch is that she was never the same.

My own "grace well" story began when I surrendered my life to Jesus in that small church in the middle of the desert, but I still need to meet Jesus at the same well every day to drink deeply of the gospel of grace.

The truth is, at some point we all have bathroom-floor breaking points when we realize that we have nothing apart from Jesus. These moments aren't a hindrance to Jesus; they're holy opportunities to bring our empty cups to him so we can be filled up with his grace upon amazing grace.

The Well-Watered Woman isn't deterred by her nothing because she knows that in Jesus, she finds everything she's been looking for all along.

THE WELL-WATERED WOMAN

MEETS JESUS

AT THE GRACE WELL

& EXCHANGES HER NOTHING

FOR HIS EVERYTHING.

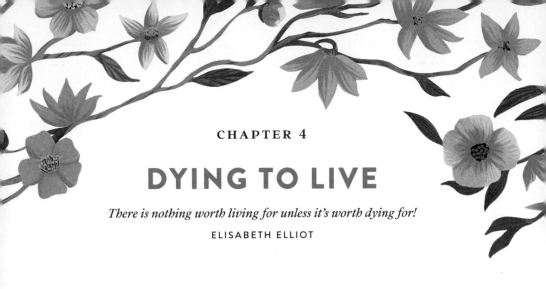

CHAPTER 4

DYING TO LIVE

There is nothing worth living for unless it's worth dying for!

ELISABETH ELLIOT

The Story of a Thirsty Woman

She was dying to live, aching to make the fleeting moments of her life matter. She wanted her time on earth to mean something, to make a difference. She relentlessly searched magazines and browsed blogs in an attempt to discover how to make her life count. She bought the latest fashions, got in shape, and saved to go on a big vacation. She checked items off her bucket list and landed a better job . . . but it all left her feeling empty. She hadn't yet learned that the way of Jesus is the opposite of this world—that in order to truly live, she must first die to herself. She was about to discover that the Cross isn't the way of death; it's the way to life.

I OPENED MY EYES ABRUPTLY, startled awake by my sister.

"I think it's time, Gretchen," she whispered as we glanced at the hospital bed across the room. My grandfather breathed steadily, with several blankets wrapped around his frail body. Not much about his appearance had changed from the night before, but my sister had a stirring from the Holy Spirit that time was short.

We hurried to find a nurse, and before long, his breathing began to slow. With each breath, his chest rose and fell with a steady cadence, as if he were nearing the end of a long, exhausting race. The nurse checked his oxygen and pulse, telling us that he might be near the end but he could keep going longer—only time would tell. Somehow we knew this was it, and we called our family to come quickly.

I grabbed hold of Pawpaw's cold, bony hands—the same hands that had served faithfully over the years, baking bread for church members in need, thumbing through the Scriptures each day, penning Spirit-filled sermons, and pouring himself out for his family and his disabled wife. As the rest of the family arrived, each member took turns kissing his cool, furrowed brow. My mom caressed his white, unwashed hair. He didn't speak a word. He just kept breathing.

Someone started to sing, as my family always does. Each person joined in like an old-fashioned choir. As tears streamed down my mom's face, her voice held a tune that soared all the way to heaven.

Amazing grace, how sweet the sound
That saved a wretch like me.

We joined in with her and started harmonizing, as if we were sitting in the wooden pews at church where Pawpaw had once preached.

I once was lost, but now am found,
Was blind, but now I see.

Shallow breath in. Shallow breath out.

We leaned in closer and squeezed him even tighter, hoping he would hold on a little longer. As we sang the last lines of "Amazing Grace," one of his favorite hymns, someone started to sing another hymn:

In the morning, when I rise,
In the morning, when I rise,
In the morning, when I rise,
Give me Jesus.

A holy hush filled the room. I glanced out the window and saw the sun stretching its rays across the horizon as if it were waking up just as my grandfather began to fall asleep in this life. We sang each line through salty tears. It was a Sunday morning, and normally he'd be awake with a cup of strong black coffee in hand, praying over the sermon he'd prepared for his church. He spent the early morning moments of quiet in the Father's presence every day, and it seemed fitting that this would be the hour he'd be ushered into Jesus' presence.

> *When I am alone,*
> *When I am alone,*
> *Oh, when I am alone,*
> *Give me Jesus.*

Pawpaw's life had been riddled with unspeakable pain and nearly insurmountable suffering. He was the son of an abusive, alcoholic father, and his brother chose a life of crime and eventually died in prison. As a teenager, he was told by the church organist that he would never amount to anything. And yet, by the grace of God, he became a pastor and led many people to salvation in Christ. After Mawmaw became severely crippled due to rheumatoid arthritis and an infection that left her with only one leg, he became the primary caregiver for his wife, along with caring for their family, managing their home, and leading a church.

His tattered Bible, held together by a stretched-out rubber band and Scotch tape, bore witness to his tumultuous journey. And yet, in spite of all this, his one desire had been Jesus. Even in his last days, when he had few words and memories due to the ravaging effects of Alzheimer's disease, he still whispered, "Jesus," and prayed that he would take him home.

> *When I come to die,*
> *When I come to die,*
> *Oh, when I come to die,*
> *Give me Jesus.*

The world seemed to pause while we sang these words, declaring Pawpaw's most earnest prayer as he took his final breath. The cry "give me Jesus" was what he sought every day. But that morning, he got to meet Jesus in a way he'd only dreamed of before—face-to-face, in what I imagine was the most glorious, joyful embrace.

THE SEED OF THE GOSPEL

Long before my Pawpaw died a physical death, he had already died to his sinful flesh. When God planted the seed of the gospel in his heart as a teenager, he followed Jesus by denying himself, taking up his cross, and embracing new life. Pawpaw knew that in order to live fully, we must die to our flesh, over and over again.

When I was seven, just a small seed myself, God planted the glorious seed of the gospel in my soul. I died to myself that day, and I still die to myself daily. But that's not where my story ends; it's where it begins.

I've always tried to look polished and put together, as if I have things under control. But if you were to peel back the layers, you'd see a different story. I grew up in the church and was born into a ministry family. I can't remember a time when I didn't know about Jesus. I've done more Bible studies than I can count, heard thousands of sermons, and read long lists of Christian books. Despite my head knowledge, however, it has taken years for what I know to trickle down into my soul and root deeply within my mind.

Even though I was a follower of Christ, I trudged through deep insecurities, fearing I would never be enough. I sought to make a name for myself by accomplishing more and being the best at what I set out to do. But it wasn't long before I realized that trying so hard in life only left me weary, exhausted, and unfulfilled.

At the age of twenty-six, five years into marriage, with a baby and a new ministry to women, I was heading down a track of believing that Jesus plus goals, followers, opportunities, and money would make my life complete. Then I had my first full-blown panic attack. This marked the beginning of the great undoing of the self-sufficiency I'd always prided myself on.

The moment is permanently seared in my mind. I was on an overseas flight with my husband and one-year-old son for a mission trip. I'd made all kinds of preparations for being stuck on a nine-hour plane ride with a toddler, but my plans fell apart when Nolan couldn't be consoled and wouldn't sleep for the bulk of the overnight flight. The feeling of being out of control overtook every square inch of my body. The world started spinning as waves of anxiety coursed through my veins.

At the time, I had no clue what was going on, but I was sure something terrible was happening. In the days, weeks, and months that followed, fear paved a path in my mind and began to dominate my life. The years since have brought healing in degrees, but my life continues to play out in the dirt and mess, and I'm finally realizing it was meant to be this way.

Living to die; dying to live. I have done both. But only the second option brings true and lasting life.

Jesus came to earth, kicking up dirt alongside us and planting the gospel seed in our souls. He got messy so we could be clean. He died so we could live the abundant life—the life he intended for us in the first place.

I know what it's like to chase after what the world defines as the "good life" and come up with nothing. And I know what it's like to chase after Jesus and discover that he truly is everything. The Christian life is about both dying and living. It's about receiving the gospel and preaching it to ourselves and others over and over again.

Lilias Trotter, a nineteenth-century missionary to Algeria, wisely said, "Death becomes a beginning instead of an ending, for it becomes the means of liberating a fresh life."[1] Apart from Jesus, we are like a small seed that lies dormant on a shelf—useless, lifeless, and stale. But with Jesus, we can be planted in the soil of the gospel, dying to sin and self in order to live abundantly in him.

DYING TO LIVE THE "GOOD LIFE"

We are dying to live—dying to grow, dying to flourish, dying to embrace joy and experience true pleasure. We ache to grasp what truly matters and live fully. But we often misunderstand what the good life really is and end up wasting our time, energy, and resources on what's fleeting. In reality, however, it's only when we surrender all to God that we can live fully and experience life that will last forever.

Even in elementary school, I felt the desire to live a full life. In my tattered seventh-grade journal (the one with "PRIVATE" scribbled across the cover), I scratched down my list of "Top Things to Do before I Die," which included (not in order of importance):

Eat a Twinkie. (*Check*. Because, really, who hasn't eaten a Twinkie?)

Ride a seesaw. (*Check*. It wasn't all I dreamed it would be— just a lot of ups and downs.)

Cry because I'm so happy. (*Check, check, check*—way too many times.)

Eat an entire pizza. (Oddly enough, *check*—it was the thin-crust kind.)

Walk beneath a waterfall. (*Check.* This *was* all I dreamed it would be.)

Milk a cow. (Still on the list. Anyone have a farm I could come visit?)

The list continued for pages and pages, filled with experiences and dreams I hoped would bring joy and satisfaction to my life. Sometime after I penned this list, a country song titled "Live Like You Were Dying" hit the top of music charts, resonating with people all over the world. The song tells the story of a man who was diagnosed with cancer in his forties. Upon the discovery that his days were numbered, he determined he would "live like he was dying" and do things he'd always wanted to do, like go skydiving and climb mountains and love more deeply.

Since it was written, this song has been sung by millions (and it might be stuck in your head now!). Though it points us in the direction of truth and shakes our temporal perspective, it comes up a little short. There's more to life than checking things off a bucket list or prioritizing our relationships. Are we dying to live the "good life" the world offers? Or have we embraced the "Christ life"—the best life, which is made possible only through dying to ourselves?

There's a better story to be told. It's the story of humankind, the story of a people who have a condition far worse than cancer—a disease called sin. It's the story of you, and it's the story of me. And it finds its roots, once more, in the Garden of Eden.

When Adam and Eve rebelled against God, sin pierced their hearts, and death permeated their bodies. No longer was creation spotless and without blemish. No longer were their hearts pure and blameless before God. No longer would they enjoy an unbroken relationship with their Maker and total satisfaction in their souls. In one act of rebellion, everything changed. We no longer live for God but rather under the rule of sin.

The apostle Paul described it this way:

> You were *dead* in the trespasses and sins in which
> you once walked, following the course of this world,
> following the prince of the power of the air, the spirit
> that is now at work in the sons of disobedience—among
> whom we all once lived in the passions of our flesh,
> *carrying out the desires of the body and the mind*, and were
> by nature children of wrath, like the rest of mankind.
> EPHESIANS 2:1-3 (EMPHASIS ADDED)

The Greek word for *dead, nekros,* describes "one that has breathed his last."[2] Every person who has been born since the Garden of Eden has been born spiritually dead. Lifeless, despite having lungs filled with breath. We're all dying to embrace true life, yet we're living in destruction and despair. Death is what we deserve, and eternal death is where we're heading apart from Christ (see Romans 3:23; 2 Thessalonians 1:9). Without Jesus living in and through us, we are lifeless.

THE STORY OF TWO SMALL SEEDS

It all began with a small seed. In Genesis 3, on the fateful day that changed the course of history, the serpent (otherwise known as Satan) approached Eve and planted a seed of doubt in her mind. He challenged what God had said and the way God designed the world. The serpent sowed doubt about God's character through his carefully crafted question: "Did God actually say . . . ?" (Genesis 3:1). That seed of doubt grew into an act of disobedience.

But right at that moment, God planted another seed. He promised a new seed that would crush the serpent—a seed that would be the Savior, Jesus.

The New Testament begins with a genealogy that weaves together the story of the Old Testament like a tapestry to proclaim the gospel of Jesus Christ. The lineage listed in Matthew 1 traces how God was hard at work in each generation. He was behind the scenes all along, tilling the soil of human hearts, making the ground ready for Christ to come. And he came right on time, in a way no one expected: through a virgin named Mary (see Matthew 1:18).

Perhaps around the same time the seed of Christ began growing in Mary's womb, another seed grew in the soil of the earth. Over time, this seed broke free from its casing, shot roots downward, and sprung up toward the sun. It grew and grew, receiving the light and nourishment it needed to become tall and strong. The seed grew into a tree—a tree that would become an instrument of death. This tree would be cut down by human hands and crafted into the cross where Jesus would be killed, playing its unique part in the story of redemption.

Meanwhile, the seed of the Savior of the world continued to grow. Here's how Scripture describes Jesus as a boy: "Jesus increased in wisdom and in stature and in favor with God and man" (Luke 2:52). Jesus grew until the time came for him to die a criminal's death on the cross to rescue us from our sins. The innocent for the guilty. The blameless for the broken.

These seeds, both planted by God, grew until their appointed time of death arrived. "When we were utterly helpless, Christ came at just the right time and died for us sinners" (Romans 5:6, NLT). One seed became an instrument of death so the seed of redemption could flourish. The tree died forever when it was cut down to become a cross, but when Jesus died on that cross, he defeated death once and for all (see 1 Corinthians 15:55-57; Galatians 3:13). He conquered the power of sin and death and uprooted the doubt that Satan sowed in the Garden.

This changes *everything*.

Your life is also a seed. Has the gospel taken root? Has there been a time in your life when you said yes to following Christ . . . a moment when you wept over your sin and worshiped your Savior? Maybe the seed of the gospel has taken root, but it hasn't been watered in a while and your faith is languishing. Maybe you feel like weeds and worries are the only things growing in the soil of your life. Or maybe you're in a season of flourishing and growing, but you need the reminder that true life comes only through dying.

No matter where you are, the secret to abundance is this: "I have been crucified with Christ. It is no longer I who live, but Christ who lives in me. And the life I now live in the flesh I live by faith in the Son of God, who loved me and gave himself for me" (Galatians 2:20).

THE GATEWAY TO LIFE

Following Jesus leads to our own crucifixion—the death of our sinful nature—but it doesn't end there. This is just the beginning. Amy Carmichael, a missionary to southern India, is said to have described dying to live like this: "I saw that the chance to die, to be crucified with Christ, was not a morbid thing, but the very gateway to Life."[3] In my own life, I've experienced the true joy that comes from laying aside my personal preferences to place others before myself. Viewing motherhood, ministry, marriage, and the ordinary events of life as a "chance to die" transforms moments of drudgery into moments of delight. God didn't create us to serve ourselves but to serve him through serving others. Jesus shows us through his own actions that death is the way to Life in him.

God often displays his eternal truths through his creation,

and one of these truths is that death leads to life. Outside my window, crimson leaves drift slowly from their branches to the ground below. These colorful leaves, dancing in the crisp breeze, are dying the most beautiful death as they surrender to the rhythms of nature. As winter approaches, the trees become bare and the ground yields no produce. But we wait with hope in winter, knowing spring will come again and new life will bud on these barren branches. The old life has to pass away before the new life can begin.

The cycle of life and death in nature reveals the secret to flourishing: it's through death that we embrace true life. Death is not a delay; it's the path to life. Though the physical eye can't see what's happening beneath the surface, new life is budding.

But what does this really mean on a practical level? Why would we lay down our rights instead of fighting for what we deserve? Why would we choose to give up what the world says will make us happy to heed the call of being happy in Christ? As countercultural as this idea is, it's the secret to the Christian life—to life that is abundant, fruitful, and free. Those who gladly take up their cross, deny their sin nature, and follow Jesus are the ones who truly live. And this happens in even the most ordinary, mundane moments of life.

When you stand in line at the grocery store only to have someone cut in front of you at the last moment—die to yourself. Take a deep breath, surrender your time to Christ, and pray for the person who is now in front of you.

When you look in the mirror with disdain and want to bask in self-pity—die to yourself. By God's grace, remember that though the outward self is wasting away, the inner self is being renewed day by day (see 2 Corinthians 4:16). Outward appearance is not what's most important; it's our hearts that reflect true beauty (see 1 Peter 3:3-4).

When your children are up in the middle of the night and won't go to sleep—die to yourself. Love them like Christ loves you (see John 13:34). He never sleeps, and he's there to listen to your anxieties and calm your soul (see Psalm 121:3-4).

When you change the one-millionth dirty diaper—die to yourself. Do it as an act of worship, a living sacrifice to God, who sent his Son, Jesus, to model what a life of worship in the mundane looks like. The majority of Jesus' time on earth (roughly thirty years) is unrecorded, yet those years mattered just as much as the years of ministry did. Never underestimate the small things (see Zechariah 4:10).

When your husband doesn't hang up his clothes, leaving them in a crumpled heap on the floor again—die to yourself. Surrender your grumbling to God, knowing that Christ cleaned up the mess of your sin by shedding his blood (see Philippians 2:14).

When your dreams are crushed and your life looks dismal—die to yourself. Hand the broken pieces of your heart to the one who can mend it and create beauty from brokenness. Even when a dream seems to be crushed, God may be raising up something better for his glory, whether or not it looks like what you expected.

Dying to yourself doesn't mean missing out on true life; it means embracing life as it was always meant to be—worshiping God, serving others, and living for his glory. Dying to yourself isn't the loss of who you are as a person; it's discovering who you were meant to be—a servant, a sacrifice, and a recipient of God's grace.

RESURRECTION IS COMING

For the Christian, death always ends in resurrection (see John 11:25-26; 2 Corinthians 5:14-15; 1 Peter 1:3).

The resurrection of dead souls brought back to life.
The resurrection of desires that bring glory to God.
The resurrection of worship in wandering hearts.
The resurrection of vision that leads to purposeful living.

The life of the Well-Watered Woman is one of dying to live. Dying to self, sin, and shame; living in Christ. Dying to fear, worry, and selfish ambition; living in peace, joy, and purpose. Dying to this world; living for eternity. The gospel song can be heard loudest in the mess and the mundane, in the dirt of daily life. The Gardener wastes nothing.

THE WELL-WATERED WOMAN

IS PLANTED IN THE SOIL

OF THE GOSPEL,

AND, LIKE A SEED BURIED

IN THE EARTH, SHE EMBRACES

DEATH AS THE MEANS

TO ABUNDANT LIFE.

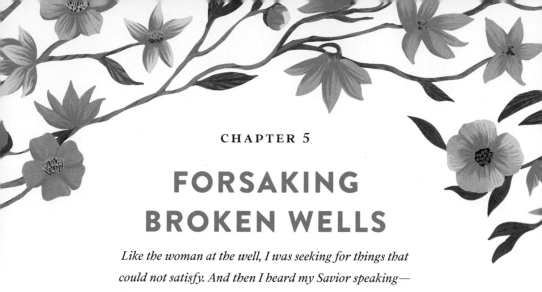

CHAPTER 5

FORSAKING BROKEN WELLS

Like the woman at the well, I was seeking for things that
could not satisfy. And then I heard my Savior speaking—
"Draw from My well that never shall run dry."

RICHARD BLANCHARD

The Story of a Thirsty Woman

The darkness began to fade as the sun stretched its rays. She grabbed her coffee mug that read, "Give me Jesus and coffee" and sipped the morning jolt of caffeine to help her wake up. The birds were singing a brand-new song, and the start of the day seemed just about perfect as she opened her Bible to read . . . until her toddler woke up early and in a bad mood. She checked her phone and saw a discouraging text from a friend. Then she spilled her coffee, and suddenly her perfect day had gone haywire. Instead of turning her eyes to Jesus, she became distracted by what was happening around her, forgetting that only Jesus could carry her through the unexpected circumstances that came her way.

FOR SEVERAL YEARS, we kept a coffee mug with a crack on it in our kitchen cabinet. Whenever I tried to drink out of it, the cup would leak hot coffee. We kept it for much longer than we should have—probably two years after the crack first appeared. This sounds crazy, I know. After all, what's the point of a mug if it can't hold liquid?

In my defense, the mug had sentimental value. My husband had taken me to a pottery-throwing lesson for my birthday one year, and the mug reminded me of that day. And after a while, the mug became a mainstay on the shelf, and I never took the time to toss it. But one day, it occurred to me that this broken mug was taking up space where a coffee mug that wasn't broken could be. This cup no longer served its purpose, and it could no longer provide me with a drink to satisfy my thirst.

This might sound silly when it comes to a mug, but how often do we try to drink out of broken wells to fill our souls? The truth is, it's not always easy to tell what will satisfy us. My mug *looked* like it could hold a hot beverage, but it leaked the moment it was filled, yielding dissatisfaction . . . and quite the mess. Just as I did with that cracked mug, we often attempt to drink from cisterns that promise happiness but yield only hopelessness.

BROKEN CISTERNS, BROKEN SOULS

Gripped by bondage and waywardness, the people of God were in a place of chastening. Their wandering had led them into captivity in Babylon, away from the land God had fought to give them. The Israelites were prone to wander, prone to leave the God they loved, in the words of the great hymn "Come, Thou Fount of Every Blessing." They had forsaken their God for the ways of the world, looking to worthless idols to rescue them, living apart from his decrees. Like children left to their whimsy in a candy store, they ate of the world's pleasures and were left sick—full yet still empty.

In the book of Jeremiah, the "weeping prophet" describes the despicable sins of God's people, calling them out of darkness to repentance and restoration. In the opening chapters of the book of Jeremiah, the prophet describes the evil committed by the people of God:

> "Has any nation ever traded its gods for new ones, even though they are not gods at all? Yet my people have exchanged their glorious God for worthless idols! The heavens are shocked at such a thing and shrink back in horror and dismay," says the LORD. "For my people have done two evil things: *They have abandoned me—the fountain of living water. And they have dug for themselves cracked cisterns that can hold no water at all!*"
> JEREMIAH 2:11-13, NLT (EMPHASIS ADDED)

Since most of us just turn on the tap and water flows out, we might miss the significance of the parallel Jeremiah is making about wells and cisterns. The "living water" Jeremiah described was fresh water that runs from a spring, the best kind to drink. A step down from living water was well water, which was pulled from the ground. Last, there was cistern water, which was simply runoff water collected into a hewn pit.[1] This "dirty water" was the least favorable, the least desirable. Jeremiah used the image of a broken cistern to describe the Israelites' wayward desires. Choosing sin and idol worship is like drinking from a broken, dirty, infested cistern; it only leads to sickness of the soul. But choosing Christ, the fountain of living waters, leads to salvation of the soul.

SETTLING FOR SLUDGE

The Old Testament recounts the story of God's covenantal love for his people, their repeated rebellion, and his steadfast love that leads to their rescue. The book of Jeremiah is set in the period of exile in Babylon when the Temple was destroyed. The people had forsaken their God for the empty promises of this world. Jeremiah revealed their two biggest sins: (1) forsaking God, the fountain of living waters, and (2) hewing out broken cisterns that could hold no water (see Jeremiah 2:11-13). The question is, How did Israel forsake the Lord?

Despite God's faithfulness to his people from generation to generation—setting them free from slavery in Egypt, providing for all their needs in the wilderness, leading them into the Promised Land—their vision was shortsighted and their memory was short term. They forgot their God and turned away from his commands, choosing instead idol worship, sexual rebellion, and disastrous desires (see Numbers 25).

That might sound like a ridiculous trade-off, but how often do we settle for the sludge of broken cisterns ourselves? C. S. Lewis describes the weak desires of the people of God this way: "It would seem that Our Lord finds our desires not too strong, but too weak. We are half-hearted creatures, fooling about with drink and sex and ambition when infinite joy is offered us, like an ignorant child who wants to go on making mud pies in a slum because he cannot imagine what is meant by the offer of a holiday at the sea. We are far too easily pleased."[2]

We can't experience God's blessing while simultaneously backsliding into sin. Like sinking sand, sin drags us deeper into slavery. God had rescued the Israelites from Egyptian bondage, but they willingly walked into a slavery of their own choosing. The people dug broken cisterns to drink from and then slid into them while digging.

WHAT'S YOUR EMPTY WELL?

Drinking from broken or empty wells is part of the human condition. Jeremiah's warning against idol worship might seem a bit far-fetched today, but it's closer than you may think—both in the world and in your soul. In Jeremiah 17, the root of Judah's sin is traced back to trusting in people and turning from God (see verse 5). God's people placed their hope in their wealth, pleasure, and false gods. Just as I attempted to use the broken mug, they tried to love God while simultaneously loving the world—an impossible feat.

God set up another contrast in Jeremiah 17:7-8: "Blessed is the man who trusts in the LORD, whose trust is the LORD. He is like a tree planted by water, that sends out its roots by the stream, and does not fear when heat comes, for its leaves remain green, and is not anxious in the year of drought, for it does not cease to bear fruit." God's desire for us is to be like that tree—planted by living water, rooted in truth, growing in grace, and flourishing in faith (see Psalm 1:3). But in order to live like this tree, we have to forsake the broken or empty cisterns we insist on digging.

We spend a lot of our lives trying to force empty wells to provide for us. Just as you can't make a broken mug hold coffee, you can't make an idol yield lasting joy. Commentator F. B. Meyer explains, "What an infinite mistake to miss the fountain freely flowing to quench the thirst, and hew out the broken cistern in which is disappointment and despair!"[3] And yet we do this every day. Our empty wells may look different from those of Jeremiah's day, but they result in the same disappointment.

Comfort

We often think comfort will lead to spiritual satisfaction, but comfort has a way of turning into spiritual complacency and leading us to the dead end of spiritual ineffectiveness. It's a downward spiral crafted by this world to make us crave the temporary and miss the eternal moments of today. Comfort seems completely innocent at first glance—just soft T-shirts, cozy bedspreads, hot showers, and bowlfuls of ice cream (all the things I run to when I just want to be comfortable). None of these things are inherently bad, but when we crave them more than a life of following Christ with reckless abandon, they become distractions.

When we get uncomfortable in this world, the only true place of ultimate comfort is in Christ. God calls us to a life of forsaking earthly comforts when we follow Jesus. Taking up a cross is not a comfortable endeavor (see Luke 9:23). Discomfort detaches us from the world and makes us crave the joys and beauty of heaven, the loving embrace of Christ, and the hope of eternity in the presence of God.

Worldly comforts always fail us. Bigger homes, softer beds, nicer clothing, and overflowing bank accounts will never be true comfort when suffering strikes and all of life swirls around us. It's a dead end. Jesus came and showed us the way of the Cross, which leads to eternal comfort. Though the cross of Christ is not comfortable, it is comforting, and that's what we truly long for.

Success

After a baby takes her first breath, the hospital staff begins to record her stats: length, weight, head circumference, Apgar score. When I was born, after a grueling delivery that ended in a C-section, I weighed in at ten pounds, ten ounces, making me the biggest baby in the hospital. Success! I wasn't even trying to achieve that award, and they gave it to me. We live in a success-driven culture, and it drives us to seek impressive stats next to our names and achievements on our résumés.

But seeking joy in success is an empty well, an idol that can't provide the satisfaction we long for. "More" is never enough. The next rung on the ladder only leads to the next one and the one after that. We strive after accomplishments in an attempt to prove our worth. But the Christian was never meant to be measured by mere numbers. Grace doesn't take statistics into account. If it did, no one would be worthy of following Christ. The only measurement that matters in God's eyes is Jesus' perfect record, credited to our account (see 2 Corinthians 5:21).

As we look at Scripture, it's obvious that God doesn't define success the same way we do. Moses killed a man and disobeyed God (see Exodus 2:11-22). Yet we look at his life as a success when we read about his faith: "He regarded disgrace for the sake of Christ as of greater value than the treasures of Egypt, because he was looking ahead to his reward" (Hebrews 11:26, NIV). Rahab was a prostitute and part of a nation that was Israel's enemy (see Joshua 2). Yet God used her to bring God's people into the Promised Land, and she is even mentioned in the lineage of Christ (see Matthew 1:5). David committed adultery and murdered a man in an attempt to cover up his act (see

2 Samuel 11). Yet God chose him in spite of his shortcomings and called him a man after his own heart (see Acts 13:22).

William Tyndale, the sixteenth-century translator who devoted his life to putting the Bible into English, eventually paid for his passion as a martyr.[4] He never saw the fruit of his life's work. Though his life must not have looked successful at the time, many came to eternal life through his steadfast obedience to God.

True Kingdom success is found in obedience to Christ, which flows from the fountain of Living Water. It's marked by wholehearted repentance and total reliance on God—nothing more, nothing less. Any other striving for success is an empty well that can never satisfy.

Appearance

With crippled hands and bent arms, she held on to a silver spoon to eat her favorite soup, creamy potato. A hard-won smile adorned her face as she enjoyed the comforting flavor. Though on the whole life had served her a bitter plate, she still held fast to the good. At one time, she had stood tall at five foot ten inches. But now she was confined to an automated wheelchair for the remainder of her days (which ultimately amounted to forty-five years of sitting). Her appearance was a far cry from the days of her youth. Now she had lost a leg due to an infection, and her hands were almost unrecognizable as a result of rheumatoid arthritis. By the world's definition, she wouldn't have won a beauty contest, but in my eyes, she was the most beautiful woman in the world.

Virginia Lee Pitt, or Mawmaw to me, counted many sorrows in life—more than the average person. Almost every empty well she could have attempted to drink from was stripped from her. Health? It diminished as her disease progressed. Independence? It disappeared as she lost mobility. Physical appearance? Even while her body failed her, her spirit grew more beautiful as she beheld Christ in her suffering.

The empty wells of health and beauty were stripped from her, but she drank deeply from the Well that satisfies—God's Word. Rather than turning inward in bitterness, resentment, and self-pity, she turned her eyes to Christ. On the very last page of her Bible, she scribbled this quote by Robert Murray M'Cheyne. It was a motto she lived out every day: "For every look at self, take ten looks to Christ." Her life taught me that true beauty doesn't come from straight teeth, a pant size, or a fashionable outfit. True beauty radiates from a heart captivated by God.

JESUS PLUS _____

"Jesus plus something" has infiltrated today's Christian culture. You don't have to scroll social media long to find a post, shirt, or coffee mug that says, "All I need is Jesus plus [coffee, wine, naps, glitter, etc.]." Of course, this is often said tongue in cheek, but there's a danger to this thinking. Without even realizing it, we often equate the God of the universe with his creation. Instead of seeing the gifts he gives us as a means to point us back to him, we buy into the lie that we need these things for our happiness. We forget that Jesus is sufficient and supreme—and that we need only him for joy, peace, and true soul rest.

We might not blatantly say, "Give me Jesus plus _____," but we often live out this belief through our actions. We don't need a whole lot of Jesus and a little bit of coffee; we *only* need a whole lot of Jesus. Praise God for the coffee, but don't allow the things of this world to take the place of what only he can give. Coffee (or fill in the blank) is a temporary fix, but Jesus is an eternal treasure. Trusting in anything other than Christ ultimately leads to endless chaos and emptiness—to broken, empty cisterns.

The list of empty wells and broken cisterns we drink from could go on and on. Perfection, health, relationships, promotions, homes, and more. Just as God called the Israelites away from empty wells, he calls us to the fountain of Living Water. And there's a blessing for those who drink deeply from that Well. As Jeremiah reminded the Israelites, "Blessed is the man who trusts in the LORD, whose trust is the LORD" (Jeremiah 17:7).

Are you trusting in "Jesus plus something" for satisfaction, or are you trusting Jesus alone? God can redeem every empty well and fill every broken cistern. Whatever you've sought apart from the Savior, God can redeem it for his glory.

THE FOUNTAIN OF GOD'S LOVE

The beloved hymn I mentioned earlier in this chapter, "Come, Thou Fount of Every Blessing," sung across the world by pew-sitters and cistern-makers alike, has a verse that every human being can sing loudly and honestly:

Prone to wander, Lord I feel it,
Prone to leave the God I love;
Here's my heart, O, take and seal it;
Seal it for thy courts above.

Robert Robinson, the writer of this powerful hymn, hewed many broken cisterns during his lifetime. He spent many years as a teen in total rebellion, seeing a fortune-teller shortly before he repented and turned to Christ.[5] Even after being wrecked and rebuilt by the gospel of grace, he was still prone to wander from the Lord, as we all are. Perhaps that's why the lyrics to this hymn still reverberate in our souls today. God continues to redeem our empty wells, leading us to the Well that never runs dry.

The truth is, you will leave the Lord at times. You'll still be tempted to pick up your shovel and start digging empty wells and broken cisterns. You may walk through seasons of sin and waywardness that shock you. But when you return to Christ in repentance and trust, planting yourself by the streams of living water once more, God is faithful to forgive and restore. As F. B.

Meyer says, "At your feet, O weary cistern-hewer, the fountain of God's love is flowing through the channel of the Divine Man! Stoop to drink it."[6]

Stoop low to drink today. The fountain of Christ's blood, shed for you, still flows freely. Set aside your broken cisterns and receive the mercy of God, made possible through his Son, Jesus.

> *Jesus sought me when a stranger,*
> *Wand'ring from the fold of God;*
> *He, to rescue me from danger,*
> *Bought me with His precious blood.*

THE WELL-WATERED WOMAN

RECOGNIZES THAT TRUE JOY

DOESN'T COME FROM

COFFEE, VACATION, NAPS,

SUCCESS, OR COMFORT.

HER JOY COMES ONLY

FROM THE LORD.

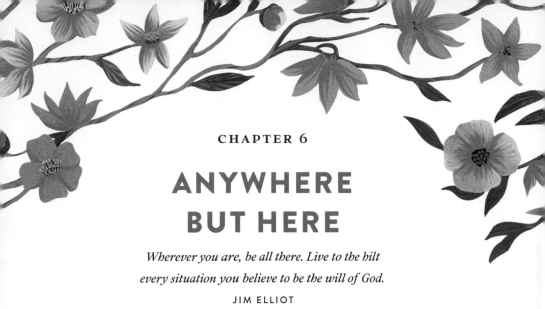

CHAPTER 6

ANYWHERE BUT HERE

Wherever you are, be all there. Live to the hilt
every situation you believe to be the will of God.

JIM ELLIOT

The Story of a Thirsty Woman

Life didn't look at all the way she'd planned. Whatever happened to the happily-ever-after she'd read about in fairy tales? Prince Charming was nowhere to be found, and her "castle" looked like a temporary apartment. Her job had nothing to do with her dreams, and she was always in another world, daydreaming about a place where life was easy. She wanted to be anywhere but here because surely if she were "there," life would be fulfilling. What she still needed to grasp was that the grass isn't always greener on the other side. In her longing to be "there," she was missing out on the green grass growing right beneath her feet.

"GOD, TAKE ME *anywhere* but here," I cried out from the very depths of my heart. Life didn't look the way I'd dreamed it would. Work wasn't glamorous, marriage wasn't easy, and my unrealistic expectations were causing chaos in my soul. We'd moved to a new city, but we were finding that forming roots was harder than we'd expected. Greg and I had been married only a few years, and the responsibilities of life had begun to feel too heavy to bear. We were past the honeymoon phase of marriage, and our plans for the future kept being upended.

We'd been in the process of applying to be missionaries overseas, but God had shut the door and made it clear that we were to stay where we were . . . which was exactly where we didn't want to be. We were trying to figure out what was next for us, but the way forward seemed unclear.

Though I was lying in bed when these honest words tumbled out, I felt as if I were in a dark wilderness, entangled by prickly bushes. Doubts overshadowed my sense of peace. The garden of my soul had been overtaken by disappointment—in life, in people, in myself, and in God. I once saw the flowers blooming on the side of the road and rejoiced at the wonder of such beauty. But I could no longer distinguish the flowers from the weeds—everything looked the same. I didn't want to be "here" anymore. I wanted to be "there," in a place of abundance, freedom, joy, and flourishing.

Why had God brought me here in the first place? To languish? To suffer? To lose my joy and passion? When the opportunity arose for my husband and me to move for a missions opportunity, peace settled over my soul. I brimmed with an expectation of the good things ahead. Never did I imagine God would plant us in a place that had appeared to be a flourishing garden but ended up being a dense, lonely wilderness. Ever since I was a little girl, I'd dreamed of being an overseas missionary. When God closed this door, I was confused and discontented. On top of that, I'd attempted to start a small online shop that was turning out to be more of a financial hindrance than a help.

Around this time, I received a text from a close friend living in a true wilderness setting in Southeast Asia, sharing a similar sentiment. "This is so much harder than I thought it would be," she wrote. "I know God has called us here, but I feel so unsettled and spiritually dry."

Our circumstances were different, but the feeling was the same: disappointment of the soul. She'd thought that when she followed God's call to move overseas and share Jesus with those who had not heard the gospel, she would finally experience the joy and fulfillment she longed for. Instead, her daily life consisted of mundane activities that were nearly impossible due to a lack of resources and the cultural challenges she faced.

Why did God bring her here? "Here" was once her "there." But now that she was here, she wanted to be in a different "there." Though we were on opposite sides of the globe, facing different challenges, our struggle was the same: *finding contentment in Christ where we'd been planted*. We both loved Jesus and wanted to follow him anywhere, but we both struggled to find joy right under our feet.

No matter who you are, where you are, or what you currently do, you've probably prayed a similar prayer yourself:

> *God, take me to a new city where I can finally find community*
> *and friendship.*
> *God, send me a husband to ease my aching heart.*
> *God, deliver me from the heart-wrenching pain of infertility.*
> *God, make this cancer go into remission.*
> *God, take me anywhere but here.*

I've uttered prayers like this more times than I can count. My "here" has changed, but the sentiment hasn't. Most of the time, I can find something I don't like about where God has planted me. Somehow the garden in someone else's yard always looks better than the one I've been called to tend. Maybe there's a drought, and my soul feels like a withering plant. Or perhaps I'm surrounded by obstacles—rocks, sand, or other plants—and I want to be free from the reality of life in a fallen world. "Here" never seems to be where I want to be. "There" always appears to be more appealing.

"SOMEDAY" ISN'T YOURS

It's not new for us to desire something other than what's right in front of us. Even Adam and Eve weren't content with the flawless creation they lived in and the open-ended communication they experienced with God. If the first human beings weren't content with the abundance God had given them, no wonder we struggle to find satisfaction, joy, and peace right where we are. We, too, are tempted to want more than what God has graciously provided. Maybe we're tempted by comparison or envy or self-advancement rather than by literal fruit, but the temptation toward discontentment still rages within our souls. The only antidote for this kind of discontentment is to acknowledge that "someday" doesn't belong to us.

Thousands of years ago, God appeared to a man named Abram and called him out of the country he was living in to go to a new place, a promised home that God would provide (see Genesis 12). God also promised that Abram would become the father of many nations. The only catch was that Abram had no children and his wife was barren (see Genesis 11:30). Despite the craziness of this call, Abram left everything to go to an unknown land with his beautiful but barren wife.

Abram was heading to the land of promise, but he had to go through a lot of unwanted "heres" first. When he obeyed God's call to go, I'm certain he had no clue where the journey would take him, the temptations he would encounter along the way, or the twists and turns he'd have to navigate before he arrived. It would be twenty-five long years of waiting, traveling, and wondering before this promised child would be born to him and his wife.

God didn't fulfill his promise until they were both old and Sarai was well beyond childbearing years. Throughout their journey, Abram and Sarai (later renamed Abraham and Sarah) were tempted to live for the "someday" when God's promise would be fulfilled, but God always brought them back to the present. At times they tried to force God's plan to happen on their own timetable (see Genesis 16). But God was calling them to be obedient in each moment, right where they'd been planted.

"Someday" isn't ours to grasp; it's God's alone. "Here" is all we have. So we embrace now, in the waiting, the wondering, and the searching. It's easy to look back at Abraham and Sarah's life and see the beauty of the big picture while forgetting they had no clue what their next step would be at any given moment. They struggled, they questioned, and they doubted, but God was faithful. He didn't always deliver them immediately, because every step was taking them where they needed to be. Where we are, right now, always matters.

THROUGH A WILDERNESS AND A SEA

From Abraham and Sarah's descendants came more generations who were never quite satisfied with God's leading. With slave chains shackled around their ankles, they cried out for God to rescue them from their Egyptian oppressors. "God heard their groaning, and God remembered his covenant with Abraham, with Isaac, and with Jacob. God saw the people of

Israel—and God knew" (Exodus 2:24-25). God knows all about our struggles, our slavery, our strongholds. He's a God who hears, a God who sees, and a God who delivers.

Through the leadership of an unqualified man named Moses, God sent ten plagues on the Egyptians before Pharaoh released them from their bondage. After the tenth (and worst) plague, Pharaoh let God's people go, and God led them "around by the way of the wilderness toward the Red Sea" (Exodus 13:18). He could have led them on a shorter route through the land of the Philistines, but he knew better. He knew the people's weakness—that they'd be tempted to return to the "safety" of slavery if they faced opposition—so he led them the long way through the wilderness toward a large body of water.

By the time the Israelites reached the Red Sea, Pharaoh had changed his mind about releasing his slaves and went in pursuit to bring them back under his control. "When Pharaoh drew near, the people of Israel lifted up their eyes, and behold, the Egyptians were marching after them, and they feared greatly. And the people of Israel cried out to the LORD. . . . Is it because there are no graves in Egypt that you have taken us away to die in the wilderness?" (Exodus 14:10-11).

In other words, "God, *why* did you bring us here?"

How quickly we lose sight of God's greater plan when a "Red Sea" of difficulty looms before us and the wilderness lies behind us! We find ourselves wishing we were somewhere else instead of preparing ourselves for the mystery and the miracle about to take place. I know I've often missed out on what God was doing right now in my desire to know what's next.

Maybe you've found yourself crying out to God in the face of your own Red Sea:

God, why did you allow my friend to betray me?

God, why did you move us to a place where my husband would end up losing his job?

God, why did you send me to this country to tell people about you, only to make my life miserable?

God, why haven't I landed the job I received a degree for?

God, why have you given me this longing for a relationship, only for me to find it unfulfilled year after year?

SAME SONG, DIFFERENT VERSE

God still delivers us from slavery, whether it's physical, spiritual, or mental bondage. He still guides us through the wilderness to the other side of glory, even if it's a longer road than we would have chosen. He still parts the seas that seem impossible to cross. And he still gives us grace and understanding when we beg, "God, take me anywhere but here."

As the story unfolds, God parts the Red Sea before the Israelites and walks with them all the way across. "The people of Israel went into the midst of the sea on dry ground, the waters being a wall to them on their right hand and on their left.

The Egyptians pursued and went in after them into the midst of the sea, all Pharaoh's horses, his chariots, and his horsemen" (Exodus 14:22-23). Even when the Egyptians came, God confused them and caused them to panic, and then brought the waters crashing over them.

When the Israelites reached the other side safely, they sang a song of praise to the Lord for their miraculous deliverance: "You will bring them in and plant them on your own mountain, the place, O LORD, which you have made for your abode, the sanctuary, O LORD, which your hands have established. The LORD will reign forever and ever" (Exodus 15:17-18). God took them from here to there, and they were grateful to be planted in a new place of freedom and fullness.

But this singing didn't last long.

Soon enough, another wilderness came along. "They went three days in the wilderness and found no water. . . . And the people grumbled against Moses saying, 'What shall we drink?'" (Exodus 15:22, 24). *God, take us anywhere but here!*

PLANT A GARDEN RIGHT HERE

I could go on with story after story of God's faithful deliverance, documented in the Bible and in the testimonies of believers around the world. Life rarely, if ever, takes us exactly where we want to go, so we might as well expect twists and turns along the way. There will be times when we just want to escape where we are in order to get to the next season. But God calls us to plant a garden right where we are—whether it's in a wilderness, in the desert, or in the middle of a storm.

God's goal isn't to get us from here to there in the easiest or fastest way possible. His purpose is to show us his goodness, his nature, and his bigger plan. More often than not, our stubborn hearts learn to forsake the world and hold tight to the Kingdom only through suffering and trials—and being in a place we never would have chosen to be.

One of the most commonly quoted Bible verses is Jeremiah 29:11. You'll find it displayed on coffee mugs, printed on shirts, and hanging on walls. This promise is packed with the dynamite of hope, bursting with color and light for the soul walking through a wilderness. If you aren't already reciting this passage in your head, the verse says, "'For I know the plans I have for you,' declares the LORD, 'plans to prosper you and not to harm you, plans to give you hope and a future'" (NIV). If you're like me, you also feel reality crashing into the promise of this verse. If God's plans are truly for good, for our hope and future, then why do they seem so difficult at the moment?

The unfortunate reality is that we don't always dig into the context of this promise. Someone told me once that reading Scripture without context is like trying to keep a fish alive out of water. We can't see the truth in its fullness without seeing it in its proper context.

Here's the scene: the Israelites were exiled from Jerusalem

by the evil king Nebuchadnezzar. They'd been torn from their homes and taken to a foreign land. God spoke to the survivors through the prophet Jeremiah, who sent this handwritten letter to the people: "Thus says the LORD of hosts, the God of Israel, to all the exiles whom I have sent into exile from Jerusalem to Babylon: Build houses and live in them; plant gardens and eat their produce" (Jeremiah 29:4-5). God's response to their predicament? Plant a garden right where you are.

When I'm in a place I don't want to be, I don't want to put down roots, and I certainly don't want to plant a garden. Gardens take work and time and patience. They represent being settled, surrendered, and satisfied—pretty much the opposite of how you'd feel in enemy territory. I'm pretty sure the exiled Israelites wouldn't have been thrilled with this instruction. God was telling them to make a home in a place they never wanted to be.

Now comes the passage we can hang on the wall:

For thus says the LORD: When seventy years are completed for Babylon, I will visit you, and I will fulfill to you my promise and bring you back to this place. For I know the plans I have for you, declares the LORD, plans for welfare and not for evil, to give you a future and a hope. Then you will call upon me and come and pray to me, and I will hear you. You will seek me and find me, when you seek me with all your heart.
JEREMIAH 29:10-13

God can take the Babylon of your life and make it into a beautiful place of revival and restoration. But first you must plant a garden. You must surrender your own plans and purposes in exchange for his, which are far greater than anything you could conjure up in your human nearsightedness.

The Well-Watered Woman doesn't escape the challenging seasons and situations of life. Instead, she plants gardens where she has been placed, just as the Israelites did in captivity in Babylon. By getting her hands dirty and planting a garden where she never wanted to be in the first place, she learns to seek God and find him in a place she never thought he could be found.

TODAY IS THE DAY

When I was lying on my bed asking God to take me anywhere but here, the Holy Spirit broke into my heart and loosened me from the tangled brush of discouragement. Conviction flooded me as this thought tumbled around in my mind: *If you aren't faithful here, who says you'll be faithful there?*

God hasn't called us to tomorrow; he has entrusted us with *today*. And today might include a wilderness, a Red Sea, or an exile. It might include a temporary home, a stint in enemy territory, or a situation you never would have chosen. Today is also a day to be faithful, to plant a garden, to hold tight to God's promises that have already been fulfilled in the blood of Jesus Christ.

Jim Elliot once said, "Wherever you are, be all there. Live to the hilt every situation you believe to be the will of God."[1] May we live this way, with our roots deep in the soil of now, whether we find ourselves in a wilderness, a wasteland, or a wonderland.

THE WELL-WATERED WOMAN

TRUSTS THE MYSTERIOUS

WAYS OF GOD,

KNOWING HE HAS

A PURPOSE FOR

WHERE SHE'S PLANTED.

PART TWO

THE WORD

In the beginning was the Word, and the Word was with God,
and the Word was God. He was in the beginning with God.
All things were made through him, and without him
was not any thing made that was made.

JOHN 1:1-3

JESUS, THE WORD, fills the deep ache of hunger in our souls. We all have a craving that demands to be satisfied, and we try to fill it with all manner of lesser things. But only God's Word can fill us up—for now and for eternity.

The Word of God is the Well-Watered Woman's source of strength and daily sustenance. Now that she has been planted in the gospel and rooted in the truth of who God is, she grows in her faith in Jesus. The Word transforms her from the inside out and nourishes her soul with the untold treasures of his promises. Just as a plant grows through absorbing water, nutrients, and sunlight, the Well-Watered Woman grows spiritually through a steady intake of God's Word.

The Bible is a treasure chest full of wisdom, a bottomless well of truth and hope. Woven throughout every page is one story of abounding hope, enduring faith, and unending love. God's words never fail, and they never grow old. In fact, the more you read them, the more you will grow to love them and long to live by them. That's the beauty of knowing God through his Word—every time you come to him, he speaks (see Isaiah 55:1-2; Hebrews 4:12).

Not only does the Bible provide a foundation for life; it leads us to live out what we know to be true. Just as Jesus is the Well of living water that satisfies our thirsty souls, he is also the Word that speaks to us daily and grows us through his grace. The Word transforms our minds, helps us take our thoughts captive, and teaches us how to live a life that honors Jesus.

Every Hour

In the morning when I rise,
In the day when I feel tired.
In the evening when I rest,
and in moments when I'm inspired.

In the times when I am weak,
and in the times when I feel strong.
In the stillness and the busy,
in the days that feel too long.

When creativity comes,
and when hard work needs to be done.
When I stop to take a break,
and when I simply come.

When I sing a brand-new song,
and when I bow my knees to pray,
there is only one thing in me,
that I have left to say.

Give me Jesus every hour.
Give me Jesus, Lord, I'll find,
that when I let go of myself
in Christ I find my life.

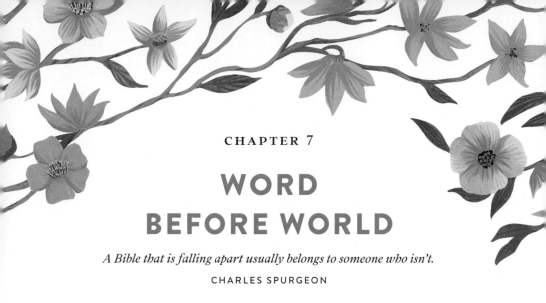

CHAPTER 7

WORD BEFORE WORLD

A Bible that is falling apart usually belongs to someone who isn't.

CHARLES SPURGEON

The Story of a Thirsty Woman

The moment her eyes opened, she grabbed her phone to browse the headlines, scroll social media, and check her e-mail. In the span of ten minutes, she stumbled across a devastating news story, a post where her friends were all together without her, and an e-mail from her boss telling her about a mistake she'd made. She was crushed. She'd gone to battle without her armor on, and before the day even began, she felt defeated. She'd been given the very weapon she needed to conquer the day—God's unchanging Word—but she'd settled for a cheap imitation instead.

HERE'S HOW I used to begin my day: I'd wake up, grab my phone (which was sitting on my nightstand), and immediately begin the "daily scroll." Before my feet even hit the floor, my heart was distracted, my soul was discontented, and my mind was discouraged. The rest of the day I'd be cranky, frustrated, and unable to focus.

Tony Reinke describes the pull of technology perfectly: "My phone is a window into the worthless and the worthy, the artificial and the authentic."[1] Technology itself isn't inherently bad or good. It's how we use it and what we consume from it that reveals the true intent of our hearts and steers our souls in the right or wrong direction. With the tap of a finger, we can peer into a window of the "worthless" or a window of the "worthy," as Reinke points out. What is worthy is what points us back to Jesus, and while it's true that good words can be found online, they can never replace the best Word—the Word of God.

REALITY CHECK FOR THE HEART

At the beginning of each new year, hopes are high, and resolutions are made. But only a few days in, most people realize how much harder it is to achieve their resolutions than it is to put them down on paper. I can't count how many resolutions I've made only to give up due to a lack of willpower, falling right back into the old habits I was trying to escape.

Don't get me wrong—resolutions aren't bad; they're a good reality check for the human heart. They urge us toward a higher goal and give us a chance for a fresh start. The problem isn't with the making of resolutions; it's with the actual resolutions we make. Most of these resolutions revolve around temporary goals, like waking up earlier, eating healthier food, landing a dream job, getting organized, or getting in shape. Resolutions are meant to change us, change our surroundings, and change our lives. But most of these commitments don't get to the heart of the matter: what we set our sights on. Most often, our gaze is on a temporary reward instead of something with eternal significance.

Fed up with my own failed resolutions, I resolved at the end of 2017 to do only *one* thing: put the Word before the world. No resolutions to exercise more, get to bed on time, put down my phone, or spend more quality time with my husband and kids. Just a single resolution to put Jesus first. Those three simple words, "Word before world," transformed my everyday routine and ambitions.

After a few months of noticing this relentless pattern of letting social media rule our hearts, Greg and I decided to make a change. We created a "charging station" in our living room cabinet, where we plug in our phones at night and don't get them out again until the morning. The goal of this daily routine is to put our phones in their proper place, as Andy Crouch describes, and put Jesus first.[2]

As I read the Word, I started doing so with expectation, recognizing that these were the actual words of the God of creation. Putting Jesus first in my thoughts prompted me to ask myself, *What does God love? And how can I love what he loves?* Putting the Word before the world began to shift my focus. Instead of trying to build an online platform, I was starting to see those in front of me. Instead of trying to be famous or do "big things" for God, I began to recognize and embrace the joy and importance of being faithful in the small things.

There are still days when I check my phone before spending time with Jesus, but I can say that God is doing a work in my heart, showing me that only he satisfies and that I need his words more than anything else. Placing our phones in a cabinet every evening is just one way we say to our souls, *This phone can't satisfy our deepest desires—only Jesus can.* It's a way to set aside what seems important to remind ourselves of what truly is important: living life in God's presence and receiving nourishment from him.

SEVENTY RESOLUTIONS SUMMED UP IN ONE

On August 17, 1723, at the age of nineteen, soon-to-be famous revivalist and preacher Jonathan Edwards penned the last of seventy resolutions he made over the course of a year. These resolutions guided his decisions and shaped his daily actions, with one aim—to know Christ and make him known.

Before Edwards ever wrote a book, before he traveled internationally to share the gospel, before he helped spark the Great Awakening, he was a teenage boy with a keen awareness that there is much more to this life than chasing after the fleeting pleasures of this world.[3] Before he did "big things" for God, he resolved to be faithful in the small things. Instead of worrying about his own fame, his desire was to make God's name famous.

Edwards's first resolution serves as the foundation for all the rest: "Resolved, that I will do whatsoever I think to be *most to God's glory*, and my own good, profit and pleasure, in the whole of my duration, without any consideration of the time, whether now, or never so many myriads of ages hence. Resolved to do whatever I think to be my duty, and most for the good and advantage of mankind in general. Resolved to do this, whatever difficulties I meet with, how many and how great soever"[4] (emphasis added).

Resolved . . . to do what would be most to God's glory. There it is—the resolution of all resolutions. Before the age of twenty, Jonathan Edwards was resolved to put God first in everything— his desires and decisions, his thoughts and time, his study and speech, his reputation and relationships, his eating and drinking, his suffering and repentance.

As a reminder to his own soul, he wrote this admonition before the lengthy list of resolutions: "Being sensible that I am unable to do anything without God's help, I do humbly entreat him by his grace to enable me to keep these Resolutions, so far as they are agreeable to his will, for Christ's sake."[5] This is where his goal setting began—and it was a far cry from the goal-setting techniques we attempt and toss aside by the middle of January.

The world says, "Muster up your own strength and make it happen." Edwards knew we prevail not by our own might but by the might of God (see Philippians 4:13).

The world says, "You have everything you need in yourself." Edwards knew success comes not from our own strength but from the Lord's strength and provision (see Zechariah 4:6).

The world says, "If you put your mind to it, anything is possible." Edwards knew that with God, all things are possible (see Matthew 19:26).

The world says, "Be the best version of yourself." Edwards believed Jesus must increase, but he must decrease (see John 3:30).

True success begins in total surrender, in exchanging self-determination for Spirit-led discipline. And true success looks very different from the world's definition.

WRECKED IN JERUSALEM

Edwards's heart was wrecked by the Lord at the age of nineteen in New York City. When I was nineteen, God wrecked my heart in another bustling city: Jerusalem.

The opportunity came up for me to minister to a school in Bethlehem during spring break, and I seized it right away. I prayed for the funds because, like most college students, I didn't have a few thousand dollars sitting in my bank account.

One evening I walked into my apartment and, to my surprise, found a pile of cash in a blank envelope lying on my desk. This final sum, when combined with the donations I'd received from family and friends, added up to the exact amount I needed. To this day, I don't know who put the envelope of cash on my desk, but I praise God for that person's sacrifice and obedience.

Instead of heading home or to the beach, I boarded an airplane to the Holy Land with a group of people I didn't know. Prior to the trip, each team member had been assigned a role. Somehow, I ended up being appointed the worship leader. My tasks included leading worship for the kids at the school where we ministered each day and leading the team in song at each site we visited. Please don't get the idea that I'm some amazing singer, although I did at one time want to be part of a Christian girl band named FHL (Faith, Hope, and Love) or Angelz in Flight (still embarrassed about that one). God had made it clear that music wasn't the direction he was leading me—thank goodness. But it was an opportunity to be part of singing praises to God in his chosen land, so I took it.

Something unexpected happened each time I led worship: the words to the songs came alive in my heart and mind in a way they never had before. As we walked across the Jordan River, we sang "Give Us Clean Hands." As we sat on top of the Mount of Beatitudes, we sang "Give Me Jesus" and "Be Thou My Vision." At the Garden Tomb, we sang "Jesus Paid It All" and "'Tis So Sweet to Trust in Jesus." As we walked where Jesus had walked, the lyrics were no longer abstract ideas; they took on new layers of depth and meaning.

The worship services for the children were held in a courtyard, with only the sky above us to reverberate our voices. Outside the gates, people went about their daily duties, some stopping to listen. With gusto and unashamed confidence, we sang,

> *Ancient words, ever true*
> *Changing me, and changing you.*
> *We have come with open hearts*
> *Oh let the ancient words impart.*[6]

I'd traveled halfway across the world to visit a place where God took on flesh, where the Word of God became human and lived among us (see John 1:14). He lived the life we couldn't live and died the death we deserved to die, all so we could have abundant life in him. Though the Word of God is ancient, it's just as applicable and powerful today as the day it was received and written. The Word of God never changes, but it always changes us.

THE ORIGINAL "WORD BEFORE WORLD"

Jesus, the Word, goes back to the very beginning. Before the world as we know it existed—before land, animals, sea creatures, mountains, sun, moon, stars, and people—there was God. "In the beginning was the Word, and the Word was with God, and the Word was God. He was in the beginning with God. All things were made through him, and without him was not any thing made that was made" (John 1:1-3).

Before a New Year's resolution was ever made, God made the world, and he did so using words. "God said, 'Let there be light,' and there was light. . . . And God said, 'Let there be an expanse in the midst of the waters, and let it separate the waters from the waters'" (Genesis 1:3, 6). God spoke, and the world was created. The Gospel of John clues us in to an even deeper level of the creation process by identifying the role of "the Word" in creating the world. The Word is God, and the Word is with God. Through words, the Word created the world.

Is your head spinning a little? Mine, too. The concept that the Word came before the world is tough for our finite minds to fathom. John goes on to describe Jesus: "The Word became flesh and dwelt among us, and we have seen his glory, glory as of the only Son from the Father, full of grace and truth" (John 1:14). The Word—Jesus—became flesh. The Creator became like the created as Immanuel, God with us (see Matthew 1:22-23).

The Word isn't just dusty letters on a page. The Word is the very breath of God (see 2 Timothy 3:16-17). The Word is a person. The Word is Jesus.

THE QUIET TIME CONUNDRUM

You've probably heard at some point that you should have a "quiet time" each day. While setting aside a time of undivided devotion to God has merit, this phrase is never mentioned in the Bible, and I'm afraid this idea has limited our walks with Jesus and our pursuit of his Word. We often assume the only way we can spend time with Jesus is by lighting a candle, sitting in a quiet place, and playing soft music, all while surrounded by commentaries, journals, colorful pens, and coffee. All of those things can be good and helpful in studying the Bible, but they're not the main thing.

The early disciples didn't have a written copy of God's Word on their bedside tables. They didn't have scented candles or color-coded highlighters. They had the stories that had been passed down from their parents and grandparents about God's faithfulness. They had Jesus to listen to, learn from, and follow. They loved the Word, Jesus, and they lived the Word as they knew what's most important: knowing God and living in light of eternity, where they would walk by his side.

The main objective of a quiet time should always be to know Christ and put him first. If the phrase "quiet time" keeps you from pursuing Jesus in the mess of everyday life, consider switching your mindset to "Word before world." If you wake up late and don't get to spend time in the Word first thing, don't consider the day a wash and leave your Bible unopened. Carve out a few minutes later in the day to spend time with him. If you're in a season with young kids who need constant attention, determine to have your Bible open continually to a passage you can run to in moments you feel overwhelmed.

Meet with Jesus when it's loud. Meet with him when it's dead quiet. Meet with him when you're alone. Meet with him in the presence of others. The Word came into this loud, noisy, chaotic world to bring peace, hope, and life-giving truth. Surely he will be with you in your own crazy chaos too! The Word of God has a heartbeat. It causes freedom, purpose, and joy to pulse through your veins.

When we put the Word before the world, Jesus becomes the main character of our lives, and we take on a supporting role. The story is about him and God's glory, and that's actually the best news to our weary hearts. Jonathan Edwards understood this when he wrote his seventy resolutions. He knew he couldn't possibly live up to all of them but that, with each failed attempt, God would show up, demonstrating his strength amid human weakness.

"Word before world" is a mentality shift, not a mundane to-do list. When you allow this perspective to shape your priorities, decisions, and routines, it will transform not only what you do but also how you do it. Following Christ is a way of life. The Word puts reality in its proper place and sets our sights on what's most important.

I RESOLVE . . .

Seek him in the quiet, yes. Set aside still moments to reflect, journal, and dig deeper. But please don't let your pursuit of Christ stop there! You don't have to leave Jesus when you shut your Bible in the morning. He goes with you (see Matthew 28:20). He goes before you (see Deuteronomy 31:8). His presence is available every moment of the day (see Psalm 16:11).

As you brush your teeth, wash your clothes, run your errands, check your e-mail, and drive your car, he is there. As you work, as you interact with the people you love, as you face joys and challenges, he is there. Your time in the Word is fuel—the gas in your spiritual tank so you can enjoy his presence and taste his goodness all day long.

Putting the Word before the world isn't meant to be something you check off in the morning; instead, it's a way of life. Resolve to water your soul with the Word each day. The ancient words that are ever true are constantly changing us. So let's come to him with an open heart.

This day, this hour, this moment, Jesus is with you. And his Word is alive.

In this world, where e'er we roam,
Ancient words will guide us home.[7]

THE WELL-WATERED WOMAN

RESOLVES TO GET NOURISHMENT

FROM THE ONE SOURCE

THAT TRULY SATISFIES:

THE WORD OF GOD.

CHAPTER 8

SPRINGING UP FROM THE ASHES

Give me the love that leads the way,
The faith that nothing can dismay,
The hope no disappointments tire,
The passion that will burn like fire;
Let me not sink to be a clod:
Make me Thy fuel, Flame of God.

AMY CARMICHAEL

The Story of a Thirsty Woman

She was burned out, busted up, and broken down. Somewhere along the way, her affections for Christ had cooled. The daily grind and mundane rhythms of life had placed blinders on her, causing her to struggle to see the beauty of the gospel around her. She found herself going through the motions of her life without passion or vision. The fire of her heart had been reduced to ashes, and she couldn't remember the last time she'd enjoyed simply being in Jesus' presence, and she missed the fullness of joy she once knew. She needed Jesus to spark her back to life again.

IT WAS CHRISTMAS MORNING, and the scent of buttermilk pancakes, freshly brewed coffee, and right-out-of-the-oven breakfast casserole wafted through the air. My family scurried around the kitchen, setting the table while listening to Christmas music as the fire died down in the fireplace. We gathered around the table, and I claimed my favorite seat—the one that looked out the windows into our backyard.

As we dug in, scooping salsa onto sausage-and-egg casserole and drenching pancakes in warm syrup, something peculiar caught my attention outside the window.

"Firemen!" was I all could muster as I stared, wide-eyed, at a white hose being lugged into our backyard by yellow-clad firefighters.

We rushed outside to find out what was happening, only to discover that the fence was burning. Before breakfast, Dad had shoveled the ashes out of the fireplace, taken them to a corner of our backyard, and left them there. Apparently the ashes were still warm enough to spark a flame with the dry brush. While we were enjoying our hot breakfast, our neighbors were frantically calling 911 because their fence had mysteriously caught fire.

The flames were quickly doused, and my dad and sister worked to repair the charred fence. Christmas went on as usual but with a vivid memory burned into our minds.

While this small brush fire in our backyard was a cause for momentary panic, fire can actually be a good thing when it comes to growth for wildlife. Contained forest fires remove decaying trees and plants to enable new, healthy growth. Fires burn away dead flora to let the sunlight in and spark new life underneath. The ashes are transformed into necessary nutrients in the soil that fuel the growth of new vegetation. While our small fire was an accident, a purposeful, contained forest fire encourages plant life by removing what is unhealthy to promote new growth.[1] In other words, ashes don't have to be the end of our stories; they can actually be the sign of a new beginning.

In our lives, God uses the fire of testing and trials to refine our souls and bring new, healthy spiritual growth. He burns away every unnecessary and unfruitful desire and uses those ashes to spark healthy rhythms that stir our affections for him. Our fiery trials aren't meant to destroy us but to grow our faith.

When your soul feels like it has become ashes, look expectantly for the new growth God is going to bring.

I LOST MY JOY

Somewhere along the way, I became just like that pile of ashes, except I had cooled down enough that I couldn't set someone else on fire. I was completely burned out, and I was only twenty-six years old. At a time when I should have been thriving, I was languishing at best.

Growing up, I burned brightly for Jesus. No matter what, I was determined to let "this little light of mine" shine for all to see. As the burdens, pressures, and realities of life built up, I grew tired and weary. I served Jesus beyond my capacity, saying yes to many *good* things while missing out on the *best* thing—intimacy with him. And along the way, I lost my joy.

It's possible to be busy doing good things for Jesus without actually being with him.

In the town of Bethany, near Jerusalem, Jesus stopped to visit with two sisters. Mary sat at Jesus' feet, intently listening to him teach. Martha, on the other hand, was filled with anxiety as she sought to do many things for Jesus without actually enjoying his presence. She lost her joy in the midst of her self-imposed hustle and bustle. But Jesus graciously called her back to what matters most: "Martha, Martha, you are anxious and troubled about many things, but one thing is necessary. Mary has chosen the good portion, which will not be taken away from her" (Luke 10:41-42).

Jesus blew on the fire of her soul with a better invitation, urging her to set aside her worries and choose to worship. While ashes are easily blown away and scattered by a gust of wind, a fire is stoked by the wind and spreads even more wildly. Martha's heart had been reduced to mere ashes as she put service before her Savior, while Mary's heart burned brightly as she huddled near her Savior's feet. Our lost joy can be found only when we return to the source of joy himself.

When we think about Martha, we usually assume her story ends there. We hear about poor Martha, who missed out on

Jesus, and we often feel just like her—chastised, discouraged, and exhausted. We want to be more like Mary, but our "doing" mentality keeps us too busy to slow down. However, the point of this story isn't just to be more like Mary and less like Martha. The point is to be like Jesus, choosing what's best in this life and leaving behind everything that lessens our love for him.

ROLE REVERSAL

Later, when Mary and Martha's brother, Lazarus, was deathly ill, the sisters sent for Jesus. Jesus responded, "This illness does not lead to death. It is for the glory of God, so that the Son of God may be glorified through it" (John 11:4). God would be glorified, even in the midst of their suffering.

The text goes on to say, "Now Jesus loved Martha and her sister and Lazarus" (John 11:5).

Martha, the one Jesus loved.

Mary, the one Jesus loved.

Lazarus, the one Jesus loved.

And you, the one Jesus loves.

Like Martha, you will experience burnout. You will walk through devastating heartache. You will be tempted to choose your to-do list over sitting at Jesus' feet. You will have moments where anxiety floods your soul and devastates your peace. But even when the fire of your heart becomes mere ashes from saying yes too much, Jesus' love will spark your joy back to life. Even in death, there can come new life.

Lazarus died when Jesus was away. When he arrived at Bethany, Martha went to meet him while Mary remained in the house—a reversal of their previous roles. Martha returned to her Savior when there was nowhere else to turn. When the fire of her heart had once again been reduced to ashes, she heard Jesus speak this fiery truth to her spirit: "I am the resurrection and the life. Whoever believes in me, though he die, yet shall he live, and everyone who lives and believes in me shall never die. Do you believe this?" (John 11:25-26).

I can only imagine the moment after Jesus' statement. Was there a long pause? Did Martha stare at her feet for a minute, wondering how to respond? Or did she answer immediately? We don't know, but we do know her response: "Yes, Lord; I believe that you are the Christ, the Son of God, who is coming into the world" (John 11:27).

After this, Jesus called for Mary. She came weeping, falling at his feet. Jesus, deeply moved, wept alongside her (see John 11:35). The perfect Son of God wept over the death of his friend. He wept over this woman's loss of joy. He wept over the brokenness of this world. He wept, even while knowing he would raise Lazarus from the dead. He wept, moved by unshakable love.

When Martha hesitated to open the tomb, Jesus said to her, "Did I not tell you that if you believed you would see the glory of God?" (John 11:40). Then he gave thanks to his Father, and the dead man walked out as alive as ever.

STIR YOUR AFFECTIONS

The truth is, on any given day, I am both Mary and Martha. There are days when the embers of my heart are ablaze and I choose to sit with Jesus over doing other things. Then there are days when my faith feels like it has all but fizzled out.

Many years ago, during a season when my heart was little more than ashes, I listened to a sermon by pastor Matt Chandler in which he posed this question: "What stirs and heightens your affections for Jesus?"[2] I'd never thought of my walk with God or my feelings toward him as something that needed to be "stirred" or "heightened." I would bite the bullet as life came, but I wasn't actively doing what I could to keep my love for Jesus ablaze. Over the next several weeks, as I mulled over this question and wrote down my answers, I was surprised to see the themes that emerged.

The gentle breeze, a watercolor sunset, my baby's belly laughter, a worship song while I did the dishes—all these were reminders of God's grace in my everyday life. Being awake before dawn with a fresh cup of coffee in hand, pausing in the middle of the day to reflect on Scripture, enjoying deep conversation with a friend, worshiping in church, reading a good book—all these pointed me back to the joy of knowing God and being known and loved by him.

I began to see the glory of God in all things, including the small things and the hard things. The joy of this realization spilled over into every area of life. I learned that I didn't have to live in defense mode. I could intentionally protect my love for Christ like never before.

There is one thing the enemy can't take—our love for Jesus. Everything else can be stripped away, but nothing can touch a heart that's set on Jesus. Satan can take aim at your health, wealth, position, relationships, and comfort, but he can't take your joy, peace, devotion, and the fire for Christ that's burning in your soul (see John 10:10-12).

Just as Jesus called Martha back to his heart, urging her to pursue and enjoy what matters for all eternity, he calls us to do the same.

PRACTICE GOD'S PRESENCE

Hands covered in flour and calloused from work, Brother Lawrence joyfully prepared a cake in the monastery kitchen—all for the glory of God. In his own words,

> We can do *little* things for God; I turn the cake that is frying on the pan for love of Him, and that done, if there is nothing else to call me, I prostrate myself in worship before Him, Who has given me grace to work. Afterwards I rise happier than a king. It is enough for me to pick up but a straw from the ground for the love of God.[3]

The kitchen isn't exactly the place I would think to go meet with God, but it's precisely where Brother Lawrence spent most of his time, and he learned to enjoy God's presence even while he was scrubbing dirty dishes, cutting vegetables, and baking cakes.

Before his name was Brother Lawrence, and before he lived in a monastery as a cook, he was known as Nicholas Herman, a peasant born in France in the seventeenth century. His first lesson in practicing the presence of God came one day when he stared at a lifeless tree in the middle of winter, looking forward to the days it would be fruitful and green again. In that moment, God showed him that his life was just like that tree— barren, unfruitful, leafless. It was only through life in Christ that Nicholas Herman would find the true life he was longing for—full, fruitful, evergreen.[4] God used this mundane moment of clarity to stir his affections. This epiphany eventually led him to enter a monastery in Paris, and he served there for the remainder of his years, practicing God's presence while preparing food for others.

Practicing the presence of God is being aware of his presence everywhere we go. He is always with us, always welcoming us to delight in him. Whether we are changing dirty diapers, entering numbers into a spreadsheet, scrubbing toilets, filling the car with gas, washing dishes, or laying our head on the pillow at night, his presence is with us (see Deuteronomy 31:6; Matthew 28:20). Jesus doesn't call us to escape the mundane duties of life; he calls us to embrace them for his glory (see 1 Corinthians 10:31).

REKINDLE THE FLAME

Identifying what stirs our affections for Christ is the starting point, but we also need to know what to do when the embers of our hearts are nearing ashes. Matt Chandler goes on to explain, "The greatest enemy of your affection more often than not is something that's morally neutral."[5] The enemies of your soul aren't always big, obvious sins; they're often just the distractions of this world.

We sleep for five extra minutes (which quickly become thirty minutes), and it leads to a rushed, chaotic morning. We click "buy" on things we don't really need, and our extra belongings end up dragging us down. We scroll social media for longer than we'd care to admit, and we end up feeling envious and discontented. And sometimes the distractions aren't external; they come from our own hearts. We harbor bitterness toward another believer, or we murmur against our roommate for not picking up her things, or we resent God for not giving us what we think we deserve. These distractions can quickly turn our hearts away from Christ.

In the book of Revelation, the apostle John wrote letters to seven churches. To the first church, Laodicea, he warned the believers against letting their faith fizzle and becoming lukewarm. To the church at Ephesus he relayed these words from Jesus: "I hold this against you: You have forsaken the love you had at first" (Revelation 2:4, NIV). Sin separates us from the warmth of God's love, but repentance, the soul's 180-degree turn, leads us back to the hearth of knowing him and being loved by him.

Sometimes we need the help of other believers to spark the flame once more. When my faith feels weak, I open up Pawpaw's tattered Bible and stare at the smudges, notes, and prayers. I flip through these pages that he pored over and prayed over, just to remember that God is an active God who is faithful from generation to generation (see Psalm 119:90). As I turn the pages, I'm reminded of the countless examples of those who have gone before me and met God in their imperfect strength. Then I meet Jesus once again—the one who is our stability in this unstable life. We weren't made to walk alone; we were made to flourish in community and in the fellowship of the Word.

When your faith feels weak, remember what God has done. Read a book written ages ago about another follower of Christ who found strength in Jesus in everyday life. Keep a journal so you can look back and recall God's faithfulness. Ask other believers to pray for you and have faith for you in the midst of your trials. Bring to mind what you *know*, and let it govern how you *feel*.

SIT BY THE FIRES OF MEDITATION

The other night, my husband built a fire. It doesn't get cold enough for a fire very often in the South, so when it does, we happily bring the fireplace to life. My two little boys are enamored with it, and I am too. The flames welcome us to slow down, to pause and enjoy the moment. Once the fire is lit and we're cozied up on the couch, wrapped in a soft blanket, I wonder, *Why don't we pause and linger more often?*

Theologian Donald S. Whitney quotes Thomas Watson in his book *Spiritual Disciplines of the Christian Life*, saying, "The reason we come away so cold from reading the word is because we do not warm ourselves at the fire of meditation."[6] If we want to burn brightly for Jesus, we must learn the art and discipline of faithfully sitting by the "fire of meditation." Reading God's Word is vital to the spiritual life, but it's not enough to read it; we also need to meditate on it. This helps the Word stick with us as we go throughout our days—and throughout our lives.

The concept of Christian meditation has been lost in a world of New Age philosophy and practice. However, all throughout God's Word, we read about the joy and discipline of godly meditation. The first chapter of Psalms opens with the concept of Christian meditation: "His delight is in the law of the LORD, and on his law he meditates day and night. He is like a tree planted by streams of water that yields its fruit in its season, and its leaf does not wither. In all that he does, he prospers" (Psalm 1:2-3). Puritan preacher Thomas Watson says, "Without meditation the truths which we know will never affect our hearts.... As an hammer drives a nail to the head, so meditation drives a truth to the heart."[7]

Meditation might sound intimidating, but it's really easier than it seems. First, set aside devoted time to dwell on God's Word (preferably when you won't be interrupted). Start by humbly praying for the Holy Spirit to keep your heart focused.[8] Then choose a verse or a theme in Scripture to meditate on. And delight in the fullness of his Word!

When I meditate on God's Word, I still my body, taking deep, intentional breaths to rest in the presence of God, knowing that every breath comes from him. As thoughts and distractions begin to flood my mind (which they inevitably do), I try to focus on one aspect of who God is and keep coming back to it, letting go of every other wayward thought. Last night, as I lay in bed, my heart began to race with problems and fears. So I began to take intentional breaths, bringing myself back to an awareness of God's faithfulness. As I breathed in, I meditated on God's *mercy*, and as I breathed out, I let go of every worry before him.

Breathe in—*mercy*. Breathe out—*worry*.

Once my heart and mind calmed down, I began to focus on a verse from Scripture, slowly breaking it down in my mind and dwelling on its infinite truth.

Think of it like grinding wheat. A kernel of truth won't become flour until it has been beaten down and ground up.

Meditating on Scripture takes time, attention, and effort, but eventually it will nourish the soul and give us strength for the day.

Meditation changes us, but the truths we meditate on never change.

THE FLAME OF GOD

That Christmas morning, when the fence caught on fire from a small scoop of hot ash, I was reminded that God can take the smallest flame and spark it into something mighty and powerful. If your faith has fizzled out and you're shoveling the ashes of doubt, discouragement, and defeat, remember that God can take a single spark and ignite it into something beyond your wildest expectations.

THE WELL-WATERED WOMAN

ALLOWS THE HOLY SPIRIT'S FIRE

TO CLEAR THE WAY

FOR A MIGHTY WORK

OF GOD.

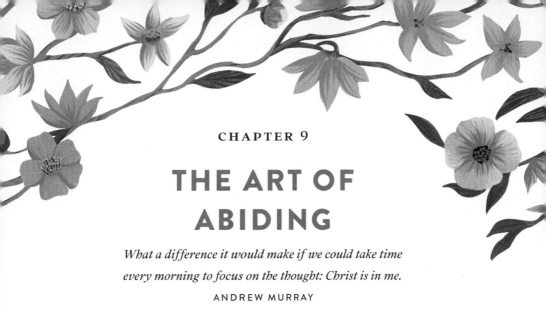

CHAPTER 9

THE ART OF ABIDING

What a difference it would make if we could take time
every morning to focus on the thought: Christ is in me.

ANDREW MURRAY

The Story of a Thirsty Woman

The days bled into nights, and she found herself losing track of time. Beyond exhausted and at her wit's end, she reminisced on the glorious nights when she slept more than three hours at a time. Her newborn woke her up at all hours, needing her attention and affection even when she felt unable to give it. She knew she needed more than sleep—she needed the help of Jesus. But every time she attempted to open her Bible, she would hear a cry, signaling the end of her time alone. Even when she found a few moments to read, she could barely comprehend a sentence. She began to wonder, *Will I ever have a thriving walk with God again?* She needed to learn the secret to fruitfulness in every season: abiding in Christ.

AFTER I HAD MY FIRST CHILD, loneliness became my closest companion. Prior to giving birth, I was positive I could handle (and master) the upcoming season with grace and ease. After all, I'd read the books telling me how to help babies sleep, calm them down, and keep them happy.

The reality of those early weeks, however, looked nothing like the straightforward formulas posed in the how-to books. One particular Sunday, when my son was a few weeks old, I stood in church with him wrapped tightly against my chest. My husband was working with the media team, so I found a spot near the back with my little one. When our pastor came out to preach, I sat down and heard a rumble from my little boy. Immediately I felt my shirt get wet beneath the wrap I was wearing. Nolan had one of those infamous blowouts all mothers know about, and I rushed out, loaded him up in the car, and headed home with tears in my eyes and a soiled, smelly shirt.

Sitting on the rocking chair later that morning, still wearing the stained blouse and with a crying baby in my lap, I wept too. My unrealistic expectations came crashing down that morning, replaced by disappointment and loneliness. And that was only the beginning. With each consecutive sleepless night and slow-moving day, my vision for "successful" motherhood continued to crash down as the formulas failed me.

On top of this drastic change in life stage, an unexpected spiritual shift happened as well. It became increasingly difficult for me to open my Bible and study the way I had before there was a little one nestled on my chest. My tired mind struggled to piece together what I was reading or to journal what I was feeling, learning, and processing. Without the time, energy, or brainpower to study the Bible deeply, I became as spiritually dry as a desert wasteland.

Desperate for some reprieve from the drought in my soul, I picked up a little book called *The True Vine* by South African writer and preacher Andrew Murray. As I slowly made my way through the words penned more than a hundred years ago, God revealed to me the secret to flourishing in all seasons: abiding.

I tended to look at reading my Bible as something to check off my endless to-do list. But abiding isn't an item on a checklist; it's a *lifestyle*. If I wanted to rediscover the joy of my salvation, I needed to learn the art of abiding in everyday life—even amid sleepless nights.

THE RHYTHM OF ABIDING

Abide is a small word with big implications. The rhythm of abiding affects our minds, bodies, and souls. It refines us, restores us, and redeems time that's been lost.

Abiding is a lot like the patient process of creating a work of art. One of my favorite ways to refresh and unwind is with a paintbrush and a colorful palette. With each stroke, the blank canvas is transformed into an image to behold, enjoy, and get lost in. Likewise, the blank canvas of your life is an opportunity to abide as God brings brushstrokes of truth to your heart, blotting out what isn't needed for the big picture and adding what brings it to completion.

In the late nineteenth century, Claude Monet was one of the founders of a style of painting later known as French impressionism. Breaking all the rules of artistry during his time, Monet set out to capture the changing seasons and flickering light using short brushstrokes and a variety of colors. This new technique resulted in some of the most captivating art of all time.

On a trip to New York City many years ago, I made a beeline for the Museum of Modern Art to view several pieces of Monet's work on display in a traveling exhibit. From across the room, I viewed one of his "Water Lilies" masterpieces. The expansive canvas revealed water lilies floating on crystal-blue water. Light seemed to dance on the surface. I moved closer to look at the strokes created by his talented hand and marveled at the attention to detail. To grasp the scope of the painting, I had to take a step back. But to appreciate the keen attention to detail, I had to take a step forward. The same is true with the art and rhythm of abiding.

We need the big picture in our walk of faith—we are forgiven, free, and made whole through Christ and have an eternal home in the Kingdom of God. But we also need to abide in daily moments—the brushstrokes of each ticking second. Abiding is an active decision to remain in Christ, to believe his Word, and to rely on his strength. Just as Monet painstakingly dipped his brush into colorful oils and painted one stroke at a time, so we abide in Christ moment by moment. Abiding is an art form—a learned discipline. But most important, it's only possible through the help of the Holy Spirit.

Abiding is not an option for God's people; it's a command (see John 15:4). But what does it really mean to abide, and how do we implement this rhythm into our lives? Thankfully, Jesus doesn't leave us in the dark about this command.

The apostle John records some of the last words Jesus spoke before entering the garden of Gethsemane, where he would be betrayed by one of his disciples and taken into custody by Jewish authorities. In the middle of Jesus' "farewell discourse," he described to his disciples the mystery, necessity, and beauty of abiding (see John 15). Knowing the Cross was coming, Jesus spoke purposefully about what it means to follow him. These teachings of Jesus are not easy to put into action. They're profound and deep—a glimpse into the way of abundant life. And they begin with learning how to grow spiritually in this life.

HOW PLANTS DON'T GROW

After six years of marriage, my husband and I were finally in a position to purchase our first house. It was an exciting yet overwhelming process, and after the closing, I celebrated by buying a houseplant—a fiddle-leaf fig. I'd seen this particular plant on a home-design show and figured now that I was a homeowner, I would naturally have enough plant lady in me to make a fiddle-leaf fig flourish (black thumb aside).

After taking this one-foot baby fiddle-leaf fig home, I transferred it to a white plastic planter. I set it beside our fireplace, right in my line of sight, so I could examine its growth every day. And that's exactly what I did. Each morning when I woke up, I'd grab a steamy cup of coffee, sit down on the couch, and analyze the plant.

Had it grown overnight? Is that a new leaf? Wait, is that part dying? Why does it still look the same?

I stared at my fiddle-leaf fig every morning, hoping I could somehow will it to shoot upward. But instead of my plant growing, the frustration in my heart grew. What I didn't realize was that although this plant wasn't shooting up overnight like Jack's beanstalk, it also wasn't dying. It was abiding right where I'd placed it. Rookie plant mama that I was, I'd unknowingly placed it in a low-light area, hindering its growth. But even in those less-than-ideal circumstances, there was more going on under the soil than met the eye.

Determined to figure out why my plant wasn't growing as

fast as I wanted it to, I consulted my good friend, Google, who helped me discover that this plant needed more sunlight. I moved it to our back porch beside a window, where the sunlight flooded in at certain times of the day. And I began letting this plant just be—watering it once a week, fertilizing once a month, and checking in every so often.

One day I noticed a new leaf at the top. It opened up and grew out, and over time, more baby leaves appeared. A year later, it's still small, but it's much bigger than it was when I got it. Slowly and steadily, growth is happening as my plant continues to abide where I've planted it.

My fiddle-leaf fig has taught me a valuable lesson in abiding. Abiding doesn't result in instant growth; it leads to slow, steady growth that transforms the soul. Plants don't grow overnight, and humans don't either. The ability to abide isn't something we arrive at quickly; it's something we constantly pursue as we rely on Jesus. It's a daily rhythm of looking to Jesus, relying on his ability, and living in the fullness and reality of his grace. Whether we're painting a masterpiece or planting a garden or growing in faith, we need to abide if we hope to experience the beauty we long for.

BE A BRANCH

The Greek word for "abide" in John 15 is *menó*, meaning "to stay; remain." It carries with it the idea of waiting, surviving, enduring, sojourning, and being present.[1] As I studied this passage, I came up with this acrostic to remember what it means to abide:

Accept pruning

Believe his Word

Identify false vines

Delight in Jesus

Endure with joy

Abiding isn't just a matter of obedience; it's the basis of joy in the life of a believer: "These things I have spoken to you, that my joy may be in you, and that your joy may be full" (John 15:11).

When Jesus talks about abiding, he is clear about the role each party plays. Jesus is the True Vine. The Father is the Vinedresser. We are the branches. "Every branch in me that does not bear fruit he takes away, and every branch that does bear fruit he prunes, that it may bear more fruit" (John 15:2).

A branch is an extension of the vine. If it becomes detached from the vine, it can't bear fruit. It can't provide shade. It can't grow. It can't survive. Jesus doesn't call you to do it all—to be everything, to go through life in your own gusto and strength. He simply says, "Be a branch."

ACCEPT PRUNING

Pruning is one of the most necessary processes for plant growth. Plants can't flourish without regular maintenance and care. An attentive gardener takes time to prune what is dead or unfruitful. While it might seem counterintuitive to cut away something you want to grow, the pruning is actually for the betterment of the plant. Without pruning, a plant will suffer. If old, dead, and decaying branches continue to steal life from the plant, it won't be able to receive the sunlight or nutrients it needs. The same is true for your spiritual growth. If you truly want to grow in your walk with Christ, you have to be pruned.

In the backyard of the home I grew up in, there was a small tree called a Japanese maple. It was a peculiar tree—the perfect place for this imaginative little girl to find refuge under its red, pointed leaves. Every spring my dad took his pruning shears and cut this tree back. It always looked somewhat embarrassed after being pruned, stripped of its branches and leaves. But my dad, the gardener, knew that pruning would ultimately make it healthier. After a few months, the maple slowly came back to life, stretching out its branches again and blooming crimson leaves as if to say, "Thank you for the pruning."

When it comes to the spiritual life, pruning doesn't just involve a seasonal cutting-back; it's a lifelong process of being emptied and filled again. Every day when we come to the Word, the Holy Spirit trims out our fleshly desires and plants truth in their place. Every trial, every season of suffering, every discipline is necessary for our flourishing. Instead of grumbling against God's pruning shears, we can offer him the dead and useless branches of our lives and trust him to bring beauty from the brokenness.

If I'm being honest, it's hard for me to accept God's pruning. I'd much rather flourish without these deep cuts. We long for blossoms without the pain. L. B. Cowman describes our predicament well:

> *Oft we run from the purging and pruning,*
> *Forgetting the Gardener knows*
> *That the deeper the cutting and trimming,*
> *The richer the cluster that grows.*[2]

So what exactly does God prune? He removes anything that causes our lives to be unfruitful—sin, distractions, self-sufficiency. He also takes away anything that hinders our growth, and sometimes that even includes good things. When God removes something "good" from our lives, it's always for the sake of something better. When we learn to accept God's pruning shears, we will be able to see him at work in all of life, even the hard seasons.

BELIEVE HIS WORD

There's a big difference between what we know and what we believe. I know a lot of things, but I don't believe them all.

I know stories about pigs that can fly, but I don't believe I'll glance out my window one day and see a pig floating through the sky! It's possible to know something in your mind without really believing it in your heart, and I find this to be true in my walk with God.

I grew up in the church, learning countless Bible verses and stories, but I didn't always believe them. I wouldn't have admitted that at the time, but my thoughts and actions revealed this unbelief. When I started having panic attacks in my mid-twenties, it revealed a gaping hole of unbelief. Deep down, I believed that God is good when life is going well, but I didn't believe he's good when things fall apart—including me.

I believed Jesus rescued me from my sin, but I didn't believe he rescued me from my insufficiency every day. I believed Jesus was faithful to others, but I didn't believe he was faithful to me. I read the promises of God's Word in a cloud of hesitation, fear, and doubt, afraid to really believe them. Unbelief kept me from experiencing perfect peace, sustaining grace, and fervent faith.

But God didn't leave me there, and he won't leave you in unbelief either.

Believing God begins with trusting him. You won't believe the words of someone you don't trust. When God affirmed his covenant with Abram (later known as Abraham) in Genesis 15, he repeatedly reminded Abraham of the promise he first proclaimed in Genesis 12. When the fulfillment of his Word seemed slow in coming, God told Abraham to "look toward heaven, and number the stars, if you are able to number them. . . . So shall your offspring be" (Genesis 15:5). Abraham "believed the LORD, and he counted it to him as righteousness" (Genesis 15:6). Abraham's journey reveals that belief isn't always easy, but it isn't something we have to muster up on our own either. It's a gift of grace.

IDENTIFY FALSE VINES

In the book of John, Jesus reveals who he is through seven "I am" statements. The last "I am" declaration is found in John 15:1, where Jesus explains that he is the "true vine." He isn't just a vine; he is the *True* Vine—the one and only source of life. The Greek word for "I am" is *eimi*, meaning "I exist."[3]

The disciples would have understood the significance of Jesus' statement "I am the true vine." In Isaiah 5:1-7, the prophet Isaiah described Israel as a vineyard. God planted this vineyard "with choice vines," expecting it to yield grapes, but it yielded only "wild grapes" (Isaiah 5:2). God chose Israel to be his people, but they failed to produce good fruit. They attached themselves to false vines and traded the provision of God for temporary pleasures. After Israel failed to be God's vine, God sent his Son, Jesus, to be the True Vine.[4] Jesus is everything God's people couldn't be back then, and he's everything we can't be now.

The false vines Israel clung to were many, and they aren't

much different from the idols we attach ourselves to. We may not think of ourselves as idol worshipers, but in reality, an idol is anything that steals our affection for God. Pastor and theologian Joe Rigney explains the negative impacts of idol worship this way: "Idolatry isn't a game; it's a suicidal reality that wrecks our souls and awakens the wrath of a jealous God."[5] Christ came to rewire our false desires and remake them into pure desires for him. Idols such as comfort, food, possessions, fame, pleasure, and relationships all promise to yield the fruit of happiness and peace, but they produce dissatisfaction and unease.

As a teenager, I attached myself to the false vines of achievement and perfection. These false vines drained me of my joy and skewed my sense of identity. In college, I attached myself to the false vines of food, control, and appearance, which led to malnourishment, depression, and hiding. After college, I attached myself to the false vines of work, marriage, and motherhood. As a young mom, I attached myself to the false vines of people pleasing, success, a clean home, a seamless schedule, and a comfortable life. All of these idols left me overwhelmed, defeated, and disappointed.

As branches attached to the True Vine, we need to be ruthless about detaching ourselves from the false vines God reveals to us. Only then will we be able to embrace the fullness of attaching ourselves to Christ, the True Vine—the only source of life and delight and freedom.

DELIGHT IN JESUS

Jesus makes it clear that we can't bear eternal fruit apart from him. One of the most astounding things Jesus says in this passage is, "Abide in me, and I in you" (John 15:4). Think about that little word *in* for a moment. Christ is *in* you right now. He is *in* you when you wake up, when you're at work, when you go to bed. Christ is *in* you when you're in a meeting, in the car, or in another country.

And this is something that should evoke joy, not fear, in our hearts. The fellowship we enjoy with Christ is a gift most of us leave untapped. Christ isn't with us like a stern parent, watching over our shoulder and waiting for us to take a misstep. He's with us because he delights in us, because he loves us, and because his life gives us life. I think that sometimes we become so busy doing things for Jesus that we miss out on delighting in him. Duty can consume our souls and overshadow the delight of knowing him.

Delighting in Christ doesn't happen automatically though; it takes training for our souls to learn to enjoy him in everyday moments. I admit that at times I've delighted in a frothy vanilla latte more than I've paused to delight in the presence of God. I have learned, though, that the more you taste of Jesus, the more you long for him. Delighting in Jesus is something of an acquired taste for those of us who are inundated with a craving for what the world has to offer. But it's possible to redirect what we hunger for.

We learn to delight in him when we open our Bible to read just for fun or when we stand on a mountaintop, enjoying his creation after a grueling hike. We delight in him when we smell freshly ground coffee and thank God for the gift of warm drinks, flavor, and trees that produce coffee beans. We delight in him when we laugh in the company of good friends or kneel with tears streaming from our eyes as we consider the greatness of God. George Müller wrote of his own journey of delighting in God, "The first great and primary business to which I ought to attend every day was, to have my soul happy in the Lord."[6] The most important delight of the human soul is to delight in the Creator.

Jesus explained in John 15:9, 11, "As the Father has loved me, so have I loved you. Abide in my love. . . . These things I have spoken to you, that my joy may be in you, and that your joy may be full." Every time I read this, I get teary eyed, because I have lost my joy in the Lord more times than I can count. Jesus knew we would struggle to keep our joy, and he also made a way for us to embrace true joy: by abiding in his unfailing love. John Piper summed it up well when he said, "God is most glorified in us when we are most satisfied in him."[7]

Are you satisfied in the greatness of God? Have you made yourself at home in his love? When we delight in Christ, our souls will be able to endure trials with joy, just as Jesus, the True Vine, did (see Hebrews 12:2).

ENDURE WITH JOY

Life will never be easy or without trouble. Christians aren't immune to suffering or bad days. As a matter of fact, Jesus says quite the opposite at the end of his farewell discourse: "I have said these things to you, that in me you may have peace. In the world you will have tribulation. But take heart; I have overcome the world" (John 16:33).

Jesus overcame what would otherwise overcome us apart from his sustaining grace. As we abide, we are able to endure suffering with joy. Warren Wiersbe writes, "Because we are only branches, we repeatedly feel our weakness and look to the Lord for strength and help."[8] That means that absolutely anything in this life that leads you to depend on the strength and sufficiency of Christ is a gift.

When I was just shy of two years old, my mom was diagnosed with an autoimmune disorder. For as long as I can remember, I've watched her suffer physically. I've seen her ache with invisible pain deep in her joints and nerves, and I've seen her endure unspeakable suffering with joy—a testament that God truly sustains despite adversity.

Twenty years after her initial diagnosis, she began to experience new symptoms. Around the time Greg and I were planning our wedding, she started suffering from extreme fatigue and out-of-the-blue dizziness. The day after my wedding, she got sick with a stomach bug and lost feeling on her left side.

This was only the start of a new downhill spiral of suffering she would walk through.

After flying for thirteen hours on several airplanes, Greg and I were finally nearing the end of the journey home from our honeymoon, with one short flight to go. After we landed in Atlanta, I turned on my phone. My heart stopped when I saw a text pop up from my dad.

"Mom is in ICU."

Our honeymoon bliss ended abruptly.

With my heart beating out of my chest, I called my dad from the airplane seat, surrounded by strangers who were oblivious to the fact that my world was crashing down. Dad tried to assure me, in a weary voice, that everything was going to be okay and that Mom was stable, but his assurance didn't settle my soul.

We boarded our last flight home to Nashville with heavy, concerned hearts. Though it was the shortest flight we'd taken, it felt impossibly long. A few days later, I packed my bags and drove back to Atlanta to be with my parents.

We returned from paradise to pain. In the coming days, I sat by my mom's bedside while the doctors tried to diagnose what was happening. She doesn't remember much of those initial days in the ICU, but I've kept a note on my phone for eight years now with the names of ER nurses and doctors. My mom wanted me to keep track of their names so she could pray for them. Even when she couldn't walk or see, Christ gave her endurance to keep loving others and living in his strength. My mom's belief never wavered, and to this day, she stands firmly on the promises and goodness of God.

AT HOME IN HIM

So what does abiding mean for our everyday life? It means we can't do anything worthwhile without Christ. It means we have all we need in order to do what he has called us to do. And it means the pressure is off to do everything on our own. We don't have to do it all, because Jesus already did it all—and he still does it all. He is the True Vine, and we are his branches.

Let's make our home in this reality, believing *Christ is in me*. This is our hope, and this is his glory.

THE WELL-WATERED WOMAN

ABIDES IN CHRIST

AND RECOGNIZES

THAT APART FROM HIM,

SHE CAN DO NOTHING.

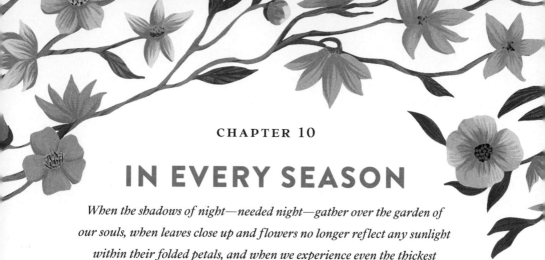

CHAPTER 10

IN EVERY SEASON

When the shadows of night—needed night—gather over the garden of our souls, when leaves close up and flowers no longer reflect any sunlight within their folded petals, and when we experience even the thickest darkness, we must remember that we will never be found wanting and that the comforting drops of heavenly dew fall only after the sun has set.

L. B. COWMAN

The Story of a Thirsty Woman

When she answered the phone, the doctor delivered news she didn't want to hear. Her world began to unravel, and the first question that came to her mind was *Why? Why me? Why this diagnosis? Why now?* As the months went on, she continued to question and wrestle, hoping for answers and for relief from her fears. Opening her Bible became harder as time went on. When she felt sick, her eyes could barely focus on the words on the page. Anxiety settled over her soul like a storm cloud, obstructing her vision. But she was about to discover that it only took a single word from Scripture to calm her anxious soul. Through that testing season, she would learn to trust God wholeheartedly and to rely on his Word . . . even if it was just one word at a time.

THE DAY MY HUSBAND left to begin a new job in Georgia, I felt a little off. It had been a stressful two weeks since Greg had accepted the position and transitioned out of his role at the church where he'd been serving for five years. Everything happened quickly, and we didn't have a chance to find a place to live in Atlanta, so we planned to move in with my parents while we searched for a home.

I had been feeling a bit nauseated and tired, but I kept chalking it up to the stress of moving with a toddler. After several days, however, the sick feeling still hadn't eased. So about an hour after I gave Greg a kiss good-bye and sent him off to Georgia, I decided to take a pregnancy test.

I called Greg before he even arrived in Atlanta. "So . . . I know this is not the best timing, but we are pregnant!" I told him with anxiety, excitement, and shock knotted together in my stomach.

The following week, with the help of our gracious friends, I packed up our home in Knoxville while Greg began his new job. Early pregnancy exhaustion and nausea hit hard as I loaded box after box, getting them ready for Greg to take the following weekend.

As I finished packing, I set aside one open box filled with my beloved plants so he could put it in the front seat of the moving van. The following Saturday, I drove to Georgia with a packed car and a toddler in tow while Greg loaded the van with the rest of our belongings. When he arrived at my parents' house that evening, I discovered that my box of plants had been accidentally packed and sealed. To make matters worse, we didn't know which box it was! Opening each one in search of them was a futile effort, so I gave up on those little plants I'd managed to keep alive up until then.

For the next six months, we lived out of three suitcases—one for Greg, one for me, and one for our son. As month after month was tacked onto this transitional period, the novelty of living out of a suitcase began to wear off. Though I was grateful for a place to stay, my heart longed for our own home. Every day our circumstances seemed to change, and there was little consistency and stability. As the baby in my belly grew, so did my fears about the future and my discontentment with our situation.

For starters, the thought of giving birth again was at the top of my "I can't do this" list. Even though it had been three years since I had given birth to Nolan, I was still traumatized by the experience. When my epidural didn't work after three tries, I found myself battling unrelenting back labor and continuous nausea, not to mention paralyzing fear. I remember whispering to my husband, "I will *never* do this again."

On top of the fear of childbirth, I desperately wanted to put down roots in our new location. We visited several churches during this season, knowing where we were living was temporary. I craved stability, friendship, and comfort, but I constantly felt unrest in my soul.

In that exhausting and unsettled season, the only thing that remained stable for me was the Word of God. When life felt overwhelming, I opened my Bible to Lamentations 3:21-24 to be reminded of God's enduring faithfulness: "But this I call to mind, and therefore I have hope: The steadfast love of the LORD never ceases; his mercies never come to an end; they are new every morning; great is your faithfulness. 'The LORD is my portion,' says my soul, 'therefore I will hope in him.'"

No move or temporary living situation could change the fact that I can be at home in Christ at all times. Even in instability, Christ remains my stable foundation. As Hebrews 13:8 says, "Jesus Christ is the same yesterday and today and forever." This truth is the key to surviving—and even thriving—in the desert seasons of life.

THE CACTUS THAT SURVIVED THE BASEMENT

Seven months after we began our home search, and as I entered my third trimester, we finally moved into our new house. Unpacking had never been so fun . . . or so exhausting! A protruding belly isn't exactly an asset in those circumstances. As I slowly unpacked each box and attempted to get settled into our new space before baby number two arrived, I stumbled across the box with my plants in it. To my shock, some of them had managed to survive!

The tiny cactus in a clay pot had fallen on its side, as if waving its white flag of surrender. But after its long stint in the basement, it had miraculously persevered on the little moisture it could find. And believe it or not, it's still alive today. It sits on my kitchen windowsill, where I can look at it while scrubbing dirty dishes. It's a daily reminder that it's possible to survive the desert seasons of life.

I've never been able to get the cactus to stand upright again, but it still grows, stooped over in humility from the difficult season it once weathered. And in a way, isn't that how it is for us? Like that tiny, tenacious cactus, we are forever marked by our times of suffering. But we can endure—and come out stronger on the other side.

SEASONS CHANGE, BUT GOD'S WORD DOESN'T

The fact of the matter is we all go through trials and desert seasons in this life. This side of Eden, sin and depravity are a reality. But we are not without hope. In every season, God gives us exactly what we need not only to survive but to thrive. He never sends us where he won't also equip us, guide us, and provide for us. The seasons of life change, but his Word remains the same, and it's his Word that gets us through (see Isaiah 40:8).

King David penned a prayer in a literal desert: "O God, you

are my God; earnestly I seek you; my soul thirsts for you; my flesh faints for you, as in a dry and weary land where there is no water" (Psalm 63:1). David knew firsthand how it feels to walk through a desert season. His search wasn't just for water but for the deep satisfaction of God's Word and his presence (verses 2-8).

When you encounter a dry season, everything that isn't essential to survival becomes almost undesirable. The desert strips you of fruitless desires and brings you back to your basic needs. In a spiritual sense, desert seasons reveal the empty pursuits of this life and lead us to the place of true hope and shelter: Christ. God's Word is like an ice-cold cup of water on a hot day. The desert reveals our longing for God like no other season can.

LIFE LESSONS FROM THE CACTUS

The cactus was built for survival in the desert. Every part of the plant has a purpose that helps it endure through heat and drought. The body of the cactus swells during times of rain and moisture so it can gather water for the days ahead. The spines serve as a built-in defense mechanism, and they also collect water.[1] From its roots to its core to its spines, the cactus isn't just unique and beautiful; it's also made to weather storms, heat, and unrelenting sun.

In our own lives, we face deserts of suffering, sorrow, sickness, despair, anxiety, and betrayal. Like the cactus, we can learn to not only survive the desert but grow stronger because of it. There are three lessons we can learn from the cactus as we face our desert seasons.

The Word of God Is Our Water

Just as the cactus stores up water, knowing that dry seasons will come, so we can store up God's Word in our hearts for times when we walk through spiritual deserts (see Psalm 119:9-11). When Jesus was in the wilderness, he responded to the devil's temptations with truth (see Matthew 4:1-11). He didn't have to go searching in a concordance for what to say or how to respond; he himself is the Word. What was in his heart flowed out of his mouth in his time of need. Though the devil tempted him with bread, power, and possessions, Jesus relied on the ultimate source of life.

When we aren't in the desert, we should nourish our souls with truth, absorbing God's promises and rooting ourselves in the Word. We can deposit truth during seasons of plenty so we can withdraw it when a drought comes.

The Word of God Is Our Protection

Just as the cactus has spines to protect it, you, too, have been given protection against your enemies. The apostle Paul shares vital wisdom to followers of Jesus: "Be strong in the Lord and in the strength of his might. Put on the whole armor of God, that you may be able to stand against the schemes of the devil"

(Ephesians 6:10-11). Paul's poignant description of the armor of God can be summed up in three commands: (1) stand, (2) suit up, and (3) surrender.

First, *stand* firm. The cactus stands where it's rooted, remaining steady against wind, storm, rain, and intruders. Likewise, we can stand firm against the enemy of this world because we're rooted in the Word. Jesus stood his ground in the desert when he was humbled and hungry. Then he stood for us by dying on the cross in our place. Because Jesus stood in our place, we can stand on his promises.

Next, *suit up* in the full armor of God. The armor of God consists of several vital pieces: the belt of truth, the breastplate of righteousness, the shoes of the gospel, the shield of faith, the helmet of salvation, and the sword of the Spirit, which is the Word of God (see Ephesians 6:13-17). Prayer enables us to wield our weapons and take hold of the truth the Spirit of God has provided for us (see Ephesians 6:18). We've been given all we need through Christ to survive the desert and triumph over the enemy, but we must be faithful to suit up in the armor we've been given.

Finally, *surrender* to God's plans, power, and purposes. We fight *from* the victory of Jesus, not *for* victory. Victory has already been claimed at the Cross. Though we fight many battles in this life, we fight knowing that Christ has already won. And because we are children of God, we have won too.

The Word of God Gives Us Roots

Every desert season has a purpose—nothing is wasted in the Kingdom of God. In college, when I was tearing down the stronghold of an eating disorder through the power of the Holy Spirit, God was slowly opening my eyes to ways he would use my struggle as a testimony of triumph. The first time I shared what I was going through with a friend who was also struggling with her body image, she looked at me with tears in her eyes. "I feel the same way!"

She felt alone in her desert struggle, just as I did. But the truth is we aren't alone. Desert seasons come to all of us in one form or another. There's no human being who hasn't faced trial, temptation, and suffering—including Jesus. Our great High Priest, Jesus, "understands our weaknesses, for he faced all of the same testings we do, yet he did not sin" (Hebrews 4:15, NLT). Jesus modeled how we can dig our roots deep into the character of God.

Roots grow deeper with gratitude. Why? Because with gratitude, we learn to receive what we've been given and relinquish what we haven't been given so we can flourish right where we are. In every season, we will encounter some level of receiving and relinquishing. But God's Word and his character never change—he's always faithful, always good. And when we hold on to that truth, we can have gratitude, no matter the season.

A FAITH FOR ALL SEASONS

God's Word isn't just for the seasons when life is going well; it's for the seasons when life seems unbearable too. It's for the times when suffering sucks the joy right out of you. It's for the times when sorrow steals your passion for life. It's for the times when loneliness leaves you feeling isolated. It's for the times when exhaustion leaves you discouraged. It's for the times when anx- iety causes you to tremble in fear and doubt. Miraculously and graciously, God's Word is the way those unbearable seasons become bearable . . . because God's Word bears us up.

Seasons of Transition

After college, I began a season full of transitions as I tried to figure out life in the "real world." When I graduated, I didn't have a clue about what I would do for a living. Even with a diploma in hand, I had no idea what to do with my life. Through a series of connections made by the sovereignty of God, I packed up and moved to Tennessee to work in ministry at a church near Nashville. That summer, I met Greg. Although at the time I didn't know he would become my husband, we were married a little over a year later. But this didn't end my season of transition; it only amplified it.

After we tied the knot, Greg and I (1) lived on a houseboat in the middle of winter, (2) slept on the floor of our friends' baby room (thankfully, this was short-lived), and (3) lived in an upstairs bedroom of another friend's house (unfortunately, their pet peacock died while we were house-sitting for them!). All of this happened within a span of two months.

The ensuing years have been filled with more transitions—making new friends, having friends move, joining small groups, changing jobs, moving to new places, having kids. Each year brings a host of changes. In times when the ground beneath our feet seems to be perpetually moving, we can find comfort knowing that Christ is our home, even when it feels like we have no earthly home. Even if this whole world is stripped away, his Word remains forever (see 1 Peter 1:25). No transition can change God's Word, but it can certainly change us in the process.

Seasons of Loss

Loss comes in all shapes and sizes, and it doesn't distinguish between the rich or the poor, the healthy or the sick, the strong or the weak, the righteous or the unrighteous. Some losses are unexpected and knock the wind right out of us. Other losses come after drawn-out seasons of suffering and waiting. Sometimes we face the death of a loved one, and other times we face the loss of our health, our independence, or our home. Loss can cause physical heartache, and it can also catapult us into a spiritual depression.

Whatever form it comes in, suffering on this earth is a given. But when we count our losses as a way to gain the "surpassing worth of knowing Christ Jesus" as Lord, we gain heaven (Philippians 3:7-21).

Helen Lemmel, an English hymn writer of nearly five hundred hymns, once heard a phrase that struck her soul so deeply that it inspired her to write a hymn that still resonates today. After marrying a wealthy European, she was struck blind. Shortly after that, her husband left her in a heap of heartache.[2] Despite her loss, her heart still sang a song of praise to God, the one who redeems all brokenness. As her life illustrates, some of the greatest melodies of the soul come from the deepest heartache.

Even when you can't "see" beyond the shadows of loss, turn to Jesus, who sees clearly all that has happened and all that is to come. Helen's hymn reminds us what to do when seasons of loss and trouble come upon us:

O soul, are you weary and troubled?
No light in the darkness you see?
There's light for a look at the Savior,
and light more abundant and free!
Turn your eyes upon Jesus, look full in His wonderful face,
And the things of earth will grow strangely dim
in the light of His glory and grace.

Seasons of Anxiety and Depression

As I replay the moments when it's hardest for me to open my Bible, at the top of the list are seasons of anxiety, fear, and panic. In the months that followed my first panic attack, I could barely read my Bible, and when I did, it was nearly impossible to focus. My journal entries were sparse those days, and when I found the determination to write down what was haunting my soul, the words were few.

Anxiety isn't a new human condition. Look through the psalms, and you'll find fellow torn-up souls calling out for God's rescue. The writer of Psalm 88 was "full of troubles," a man of "no strength" (verses 3, 4). He wrote from the depth of a spiritual pit, overwhelmed with worries and burdened beyond belief. This psalm begins and ends in darkness, and yet God—knowing seasons of heaviness come on us all—inspired it to be part of the Word.

In the midst of our dark moments, God is near, and he is faithful to listen. He delivers us and sets us free from the turmoil of despair and anxiety. The dark night of the soul is real and can feel consuming, but the sun always rises again. The clouds always clear away and reveal that the Son never stopped shining in the first place. Though we may not be able to see or feel the nearness of God for a time, he will soon lift the veil and our vision will return—and along with it, healing, wholeness, and freedom.

So how do you read your Bible in these dark seasons? To be quite honest, Bible study in those times will look different than it does in seasons of flourishing, and that's okay. The Lord knows where we are, and he is more than able to provide us with what we need. Sometimes all you can do in difficult times is to *listen* to the Word. As Romans 10:17 says, faith comes from hearing, and hearing from the Word of God. Listening to the Word through a Bible app on your phone can open the eyes of your heart and calm your troubled soul. Other times, you might stay in one passage or one verse for days and weeks in a row, praying it, writing it down repeatedly, and claiming it over the present darkness. And other times, you might stick with a book of the Bible (yes, even one that might not seem "applicable" to your situation) and keep studying it because all of God's Word is living and active. The point is we need the light of God's Word in dark seasons, too, even if we receive it differently than we would in seasons of flourishing.

And sometimes in those seasons, you take a step back to reevaluate your life and dig deeper into the root of the anxiety or depression. One thing is certain: whether we're at the heights or the depths, we can set our hearts on God's glory and preach the truth to our souls, just as the psalmists did. This is what brought them to the other side of their despair.

Seasons of Wandering

For forty years, God allowed the Israelites to wander in the wilderness. In the process, he taught them to long for something better than food, a home, and worldly possessions. God knows that in our wilderness moments, what we really need isn't answers, relief, or things—we need him. He fed the Israelites with manna so they would know that "man does not live by bread alone, but man lives by every word that comes from the mouth of the LORD" (Deuteronomy 8:3). *Could it be that our wilderness seasons of life are actually a blessing to teach us that nothing will satisfy us other than the life-giving, eternal words that come from the mouth of the Lord?* No season is wasted. No wandering is aimless. The Lord uses every season to teach us to hunger for something better and to teach us that he alone satisfies.

In your wilderness season, know that he is enough. His Word is your shelter, your sustenance. In those times when it's hardest to open the Word and pray, God is teaching you that nothing in this world will sustain your heart; only he will. He will provide you with "grace manna" in the Word—just enough strength for each day. Let the wilderness be an opportunity to fall on your knees and remember that he will provide for you— and that he loves you with an everlasting love.

Seasons of Busyness

Martin Luther is believed to have said, "I have so much to do that I shall spend the first three hours in prayer." That's pretty much the opposite of our instinct when we're walking through seasons of busyness, but I believe Luther was onto something there. We can't survive seasons of busyness without being attached to the Vine, the source of life. When we're tempted to believe we're too busy to be in the Word, we should check our busyness and reorient our priorities so we can put first things first.

As C. S. Lewis said, "You can't get second things by putting them first. You can get second things only by putting first things first."[3] In other words, when we place "second things" (the things of this world) as our priority before Christ, we will reap a harvest of second things. We won't reap the peace, joy, and fulfillment that can only be found in Jesus. The second things of this world can be more fully enjoyed when our true enjoyment is in Christ. What you put your time into is what you will reap. When Christ is not front and center, everything else falls apart.

In seasons of busyness, it's important to evaluate our souls as well as our schedules. What can we set aside in order to set our Savior in front of us? What "second thing" can we let go of in order to linger longer in God's presence?

Once you've completed a survey of your soul, surrender your season to the Lord. Some seasons are naturally busier than others, and nothing can be done to change that. For instance, the early years of motherhood will inevitably be filled with late nights, long mornings, and hectic days. Being a mom is a full-time, around-the-clock job. However, there are creative ways to be in the Word even in the midst of a busy season.

If you aren't able to have a leisurely time of studying Scripture, you can choose one passage to memorize and meditate on as a way to bring God's Word with you all day. Say it out loud to your children. Write it on a Post-it Note and stick it where you spend a lot of time—the laundry room, the kitchen sink, the kids' bathroom. Put first things first to fight the lie that you don't have the time to be in the Word. You'll never regret spending time in God's Word, but you will regret neglecting to fill your soul with the one thing that will carry you through busy seasons.

Seasons of Loneliness

One of the most convincing lies Satan will tell you is that you're alone—that you're the only one walking through this trial and you're the exception to God's faithfulness. It's true that loneliness can make it hard to dig into the Word, but it can also be the catalyst for spiritual growth when you're forced to see Christ as your true companion.

When I started my first job at a church after college, I found myself in a new city. Although several interns moved to the area around the same time, I constantly battled intense feelings of loneliness as I navigated life as a single girl working in my first full-time postgraduate job. Looking back, I remember the sting of loneliness, but I also remember the sweet moments I spent with the Lord in prayer, worship, and surrender.

We would never choose loneliness, but it offers its own gifts. It forces us to dig our roots deep, right where we've been planted.

GOD IS IN EVERY SEASON

God is the maker of the seasons. Though your time in the Word might look different depending on your life stage, you can still be deeply rooted in Christ, whether you find yourself in the desert or the storm, in the wilderness or the harvest, in a time of change or of monotony, in a season of joy or of loss.

Solomon says, "For everything there is a season, and a time for every matter under heaven" (Ecclesiastes 3:1). He goes on with a long list of the ups and downs of life, explaining that there is a time for everything, so we shouldn't be surprised when we're greeted by seasons of mourning, hardship, suffering, and silence. But here's where we can land in every season: "I have seen the business that God has given to the children of man to be busy with. *He has made everything beautiful in its time.* Also, he has put eternity into man's heart, yet so that he cannot find out what God has done from the beginning to the end" (Ecclesiastes 3:10-11, emphasis added).

Everything beautiful in its time. In the light of redemption, seasons of loss, transition, suffering, anxiety, depression, busyness, and loneliness will all be made beautiful. For now, though, we live with eternity driving our hearts back to the Cross.

There's beauty to be found in every desert. We just need the spiritual eyes to see it and the heart to long for it—and these can only be cultivated by being in the Word in every season.

THE WELL-WATERED WOMAN

STORES THE WORD

IN HER HEART,

KNOWING THAT GOD HAS

PROVIDED EVERYTHING SHE NEEDS

TO GROW, BLOOM, AND FLOURISH

EVEN IN THE MIDST

OF THE DESERT SEASONS.

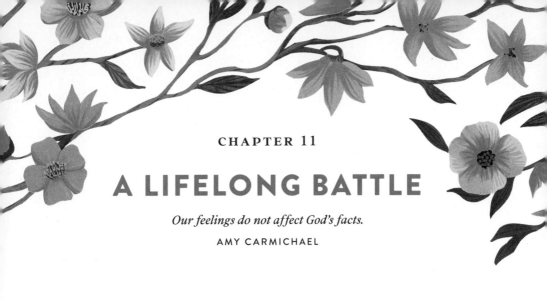

CHAPTER 11

A LIFELONG BATTLE

Our feelings do not affect God's facts.

AMY CARMICHAEL

The Story of a Thirsty Woman

She jolted upright from her disturbing dream, her mind racing like an out-of-control car. She hadn't even gotten out of bed, and already the lies were taunting her. Her dreams only unveiled more fears, worries, and stress. As the day wore on, the battle in her mind raged stronger. Fears hounded her peace, and memories of past failure crowded out the grace she longed to hold onto. She needed to make the lies bow down to Jesus, the real King of her heart. She was engaged in a battle for her mind, and if she was going to win, she needed to bring her thoughts into submission to Christ—day after day, moment by moment.

THE FIRST TIME I planted a garden, I had no clue I was going to war. I'd envisioned juicy tomatoes for making fresh salsa, spicy banana peppers for canning, and crunchy okra for roasting. That vision mirrored what I'd seen in *The Secret Garden*, a movie I'd watched on repeat when I was a girl. My daydreams didn't include a constant fight against pests and plant disease.

Not long after my tomatoes started growing, I noticed holes in the leaves. Sure enough, tiny critters were trying to invade my plants. This was only the start though. My hanging basket of strawberries became a feast for the birds, and my squash plants became a home for unwanted bugs.

Suddenly, growing a garden was no longer a fun little dream project but a daily battle against invasive creatures. I hadn't prepared myself for this war. Unsure of what to do, I ended up going to a plant nursery to arm myself with insect sprays. I was going to fight for my garden! But I was at a disadvantage—the enemy had already claimed territory I would never be able to recover.

After months of engaging in battle, I finally gave in to the garden pests. My zucchini and yellow squash plants began to rot and never produced a good harvest. The bugs had a picnic on their vines and leaves. I learned the hard way that in order to grow good things, whether in the ground or in our souls, we have to go to battle. If we enter the day unprepared, the yield will be minimal. Like the critters that feasted on the fruit of my labor, the lies of the enemy can invade our minds and choke out good fruit. The battle is won only when we prepare ourselves for war, arm ourselves with truth, and get ready to fight the good fight of faith.

THE BATTLEGROUND OF YOUR MIND

The greatest battle you will fight each day begins in your mind, in the battle for your thoughts. Like a persistent garden pest, the enemy does everything and anything he can to knock you off your feet. The battle for your thoughts might be unseen to the human eye, but it's completely unveiled before the eyes of God. And with God's unequaled strength, this battle can end in victory.

The tone of the Creation story shifts when the serpent, Satan, comes onto the scene. The first words he said to the woman, Eve, are indicative of the way he deals with us today: "Did God actually say . . . ?" (Genesis 3:1). His tactics haven't changed—he continues to tempt us to doubt God and question his goodness, truth, and love.

The enemy tempted Eve by messing with her mind. He pushed and pulled at the truths God had revealed to Adam and Eve, and he twisted them just enough to tempt her to believe a lie and act on it. Eve rebelled against God's command, and Adam joined her. Doubt led to unbelief, which led to rebellion, a cover-up, and an attempt to deceive God. Satan thought he won that battle in the Garden, but he failed to see the big picture.

God, the ultimate Gardener, steps in to fight the battle for them. He doesn't leave them to fight alone, just like he doesn't leave us. He says to the serpent, "*I* will put enmity between you and the woman, and between your offspring and her offspring; he shall bruise your head, and you shall bruise his heel" (Genesis 3:15, emphasis added). God says, "*I* will," not "Adam, you go do this" or "Eve, repair what you broke."

From the very beginning, it's God who saves the day. It's his Word that is the final say. Apart from God, Adam and Eve (and every human being since, including you and me), could not win the war Satan started in the Garden. But because of Christ's death and resurrection, victory has been secured for us. And the Holy Spirit gives us the wisdom we need to fight the daily battle that will wage until Christ returns.

NO LONGER VICTIMS

Here's a glimpse into the raging battle within:

> We are human, but we don't wage war as humans do.
> We use God's mighty weapons, not worldly weapons,
> to knock down the strongholds of human reasoning
> and to destroy false arguments. We destroy every proud
> obstacle that keeps people from knowing God. We
> capture their rebellious thoughts and teach them to
> obey Christ.
>
> 2 CORINTHIANS 10:3-5, NLT

We are humans fighting a war, but we don't fight the way humans fight. This battle is for the human soul, and it happens at a cosmic level. We fight with God's weapons, and his weapons will prevail. The apostle Paul describes the war we're engaged in as not being against "flesh and blood, but against the rulers, against the authorities, against the cosmic powers over this present darkness, against the spiritual forces of evil in the heavenly places" (Ephesians 6:12). Did you catch that? The war isn't against your friend, your husband, your neighbor, or your family member. It's a battle against "this present darkness"—it's a spiritual war that can be seen only by the eyes of the heart.

Romans 8:37-39 shines a light on our position in this fight as blood-bought children of God:

> In *all these things* we are more than conquerors through him who loved us. For I am sure that neither death nor life, nor angels nor rulers, nor things present nor things to come, nor powers, nor height nor depth, nor anything else in all creation, will be able to separate us from the love of God in Christ Jesus our Lord. (Emphasis added)

In trials, in distress, in danger, we are "more than conquerors through him who loved us."

In the face of whatever we're up against—uncertainty,

discomfort, longing, or pain—we will prevail through Christ! We are not defenseless; we are not hopeless. Through Christ, we don't have to live as victims of Satan, our circumstances, or our wayward thoughts. We are victors through *the* Victor.

Although we're engaged in a war of eternal scope, we often don't view it as a battle. Either we give in to our enemy out of fear or we don't fight because we don't take it seriously. To fight successfully, we have to know what's happening in the first place—and how all this will end. Christ has made it clear that if we are in him, we are no longer victims; we are victorious: "Thanks be to God, who gives us the victory through our Lord Jesus Christ" (1 Corinthians 15:57).

TRUTH WITH A CAPITAL *T*

After my first panic attack, I spiraled into an abyss of despair. How could I, a Christian of almost twenty years, be battling crippling fear, dark depression, and wayward thoughts? I was weak, exhausted, and hungry for truth.

When I looked at myself in the mirror, I saw several "truths" about my life: I was broken, I was discouraged, I was having panic attacks, and I didn't know what to do. These facts were the only reality I could see when darkness hid the face of God. Lies became deeply rooted in my soul, choking out the good fruit of truth.

But slowly, throughout this season, God taught me the

difference between "little *t*" truth (the convincing lies of Satan) and Truth with a capital *T*, which brings freedom. "Little *t*" truth says cancer will be the end of your story. The tests have been run and the diagnosis is certain. "Capital *T*" Truth says Christ has defeated the power of death and one day all sickness will be wiped away (see Revelation 21:4). You are strong in him when you are weak, and you are healed from the greater disease of sin (see 2 Corinthians 12:9-10). God won't leave you or forsake you in this trial, and he will help you endure (see Deuteronomy 31:6).

"Little *t*" truth says you're trapped by panic attacks and fear. You'll be embarrassed by your brokenness, and you'll never recover. "Capital *T*" Truth says that God is bigger than anything we fear in this life (see Isaiah 41:10). We are held by the everlasting arms of God, and we aren't defined by anxiety (see Deuteronomy 33:27). We are free in him (see John 8:32; Galatians 5:1).

"Little *t*" truth says your bank account is running low and you won't be able to provide for your family. "Capital *T*" Truth says God owns the cattle on a thousand hills and will provide for you as you trust in him (see Psalm 50:10; Proverbs 3:5-6).

God's Word counteracts the lies that fill our minds. The bottom line is that God's "capital *T*" Truth prevails when the enemy knocks you down and tries to deceive you, discourage you, and defeat you.

PREACH TRUTH TO YOURSELF

The lies in our minds are constantly at odds with the truth, promises, and provision of God's Word. If the thoughts that run through our minds were to be displayed on a screen for all to see, I imagine a few of the recurring ones would be

I'm a failure.
I'm a disappointment.
I can't do this.
I'll never be free.

These thoughts create deep grooves in our minds, but they're not too deep for Christ's truth to redirect. Paul urges in Romans 12:2, "Do not be conformed to this world, but be *transformed* by the renewal of your mind, that by testing you may discern what is the will of God, what is good and acceptable and perfect" (emphasis added). The Greek word for *transform, anakainōsis*, refers to "a renewal or change of heart and life."[1] God's Word ultimately rewires our hearts and minds so they're focused on what's eternal instead of driven by what's temporary. God's Word plants truth and uproots lies. It clears pathways for renewal, and it covers up pathways that block peace. The key that will set you free is knowing God's Word inside and out.

The way to change your thoughts is through the daily discipline of preaching truth to your heart. In order to be a truth preacher, you have to know the pathways in your mind that are in need of rewiring, and you need to know the truth. Then you'll be able to pave new ways of thinking.

Jesus made it clear that knowing Truth with a capital *T* brings freedom (see John 8:36). The truth of the gospel, the truth of his love for us, the truth of new life in him—these aren't messages we need to hear just once in order to be set free. They're realities we need to be reminded of over and over again.

Your thoughts might tell you, *I'm broken. I don't have value. I'm a fraud.* But the truth of God's Word says, "I'm redeemed through Christ. I'm a new creation. I'm called and equipped to live for his glory" (see Romans 3:24; 2 Corinthians 5:17; 2 Peter 1:3).

Your thoughts might say, *I can't do this. I can't flourish in the face of trials.* But the truth of God's Word says, "I have all I need in Christ. I can do exactly what he calls me to do through his strength" (see Philippians 4:13, 19).

Your thoughts might say, *I can never be free. I will always be in bondage to fear and anxiety.* But the truth of God's Word says, "It is for freedom that Christ has set me free! His peace is possible in all circumstances" (see Galatians 5:1; Philippians 4:4-9).

Elyse Fitzpatrick writes,

When your heart accuses you and says, "You're so worthless. Look at the way you've failed him again!" you can confidently answer, "It is true that on my own I am worthless, but he has made me completely righteous in his Son. He has declared that he loves me and his love is now the most important thing about me. I believe that he won't stop loving me until he stops loving his own Son. I can begin to serve him again because I know he is here, with me, sustaining me and granting me his grace."[2]

This is how you preach Truth with a capital *T* to your mind. When the enemy tries to drag you down through lies, doubts, and wayward thoughts, petition the Father to plant his truth deeper into your heart. The words you think impact how you talk, live, love, make decisions, and approach trials. Thoughts are ultimately made up of words, and words have more power than we realize. The good news is that God's Word has the ultimate authority over any word and thought.

GOD'S WORD AS A WEAPON

I used to have a hard time separating the lies of the enemy from the truths of God's Word. The lies were loud, and I allowed myself to be deceived by their threats. The reality of this stronghold became the most evident when I began working in women's ministry.

Leading others always exposes what we really believe about God and his Word. What comes out of our mouths is first sown and rooted in our hearts (see Luke 6:45). My words, thoughts, and feelings revealed what I truly believed, and my doubts about God's Word became more and more obvious. Not long after I began a small business with the sole aim of equipping women to know Jesus more through the Word, I realized how little I actually believed in Scripture. I would have said it was true, but I hadn't fully bought into how it was true for my own day-to-day reality.

After the onset of my panic attacks, I had to take a leave of absence from ministry to rest, seek counseling, root myself in the Word, and reevaluate my goals and priorities. It was during this dark, lonely season that the identity of being a "failure" was tattooed on my heart. I felt like I'd failed as a Christian and as a follower of Jesus. The enemy was sabotaging my identity in Christ, and I didn't know how to fight back.

During that season, I read a quote by Martyn Lloyd-Jones that changed everything for me: "Most of your unhappiness in life is due to the fact that you are listening to yourself instead of talking to yourself."[3] When I listened to the lies of the enemy, I spiraled into defeat. But when I preached to myself, reminding my soul of God's unfailing truth, I was able to stand firm in confidence (see Psalm 42:5).

There were moments in that dark season when I wanted to quit ministry altogether. My failures were so glaring that I felt disqualified from sharing about Jesus with others. But since listening to the lies of the enemy was clearly not making life any better, I decided to take Martyn Lloyd-Jones's advice and start talking back to my soul with truth. Instead of wallowing in the idea that I was a failure, I started memorizing 2 Corinthians 12:9-10 and reciting to myself that God's strength is made perfect in my weakness.

I would scribble this reminder on my hand so I could see it throughout the day. I'd write it on a notecard so I could take it with me whenever I needed it. Instead of quitting ministry in defeat, I decided to quit believing the enemy's lies. I quit trying to be perfect. I quit trying to impress other people. Eventually God transformed my view of failure and showed me that his strength is always available in my weakness and that his rescue is imminent.

God doesn't call us to quit fighting the war for our minds, but he does call us to quit fighting it in our own strength. He has given us the weapon we need to experience victory—the Word of God. And we should preach this "capital *T*" truth to our souls every day.

YOU WIN BECAUSE HE WON

The ministry and life of Jesus was full of words, and every one of them held power. We have his Word today, and we have the entire canon of Scripture, from Genesis to Revelation, at our fingertips! These words aren't mere ink on a page. They have a heartbeat; they are pulsing with life. They tell the truth, and they show the way to victory—through Christ alone.

If you want to be a fighter in the cosmic spiritual battle and a Well-Watered Woman in a dried-up world, you have to fully rely on Jesus and know his Word. You'll want to give in at times because your feelings yell louder than your faith. You'll have days you trip into the pit and don't realize it until everything gets dark and you have to yell for help. But you don't have to fight this battle wondering what the outcome will be.

You can fight from Jesus' victory.

When the apostle John was exiled on the island of Patmos, he received from Jesus a revelation of the end times and recorded it in what became the book of Revelation—the last words of Scripture. Throughout this book, we see the final cosmic battle unfold, when the enemy will be defeated forever and Christ will be exalted on his throne. Right before Satan's ultimate defeat, Jesus is seen sitting on a white horse. He is "Faithful and True, and in righteousness he judges and makes war. . . . He is clothed in a robe dipped in blood, and the name by which he is called is The Word of God" (Revelation 19:11, 13).

Jesus, the Word, has won the war. The enemy's end is coming and has been set in stone. One day Satan will be cast into the lake of fire, and Christ will be seated on his throne forever (see Revelation 5:13; 11:15; 20:10).

So fight the battle for your mind with confidence, knowing that you will win because Jesus already won. It's "capital *T*" Truth that leads to a life of victory.

THE WELL-WATERED WOMAN

TAKES HER WAYWARD

THOUGHTS CAPTIVE,

CONFORMING THEM

TO THE WAYS OF JESUS.

PART THREE

THE WAY

*The righteous flourish like the palm tree and grow like a cedar in
Lebanon. They are planted in the house of the LORD; they flourish in the
courts of our God. They still bear fruit in old age; they are ever full of sap
and green, to declare that the LORD is upright; he is my rock,
and there is no unrighteousness in him.*

PSALM 92:12-15

JESUS, THE WAY, guides us every step of our journey of following him. Through his life, we are invited to flourish right where we're planted. He leads us through valleys, loves us through hardship, and lifts us up when we are weak.

The way of Jesus is the way to a life that blooms and flourishes. Growth in the Christian life always leads to abundance. But it doesn't necessarily look like the world's definition of abundance. Scripture is clear that we've been saved by grace through faith in Jesus (see Ephesians 2:8-9). It's by God's grace that we are planted and rooted in the soil of the gospel. It's through faith that we continue to grow in him. And it's God's grace that shapes the way we live and what we do with our lives. We have been created by God to follow the way of Jesus and to walk out our faith in our everyday life (see Ephesians 2:10).

The way of Jesus is worked out in everyday obedience. The gospel is not Good News only on the day of our salvation; it's Good News every day, and it propels us forward in faith. Following Jesus, the Way, affects how we live, make decisions, and perceive our present suffering. It revolutionizes our goals and dreams and renews our vision when we face adversity. It's seen in the way we serve others, love others, and use our time. It's evident in our ambitions, our plans, and our pursuits. The Well-Watered Woman follows the way of Jesus. She blooms for God's glory as she faithfully follows him, and she flourishes as she shares the gospel with others through both her words and her actions.

Follow the Way

Which way do I go?
Which steps do I take?
What if I take the wrong road
Or make a tragic mistake?

Or follow the wrong voice
And walk the wrong path?
Or choose the wrong choice . . .
And left with the aftermath?

These questions keep swirling,
making me dizzy with fear.
You gently call me, saying,
"Come and draw near."

Follow the Way
that Jesus went—
The Way of the cross,
The Way of a life well spent.

The Way of Jesus
is a narrow road.
But when you travel on it,
it will take you home.

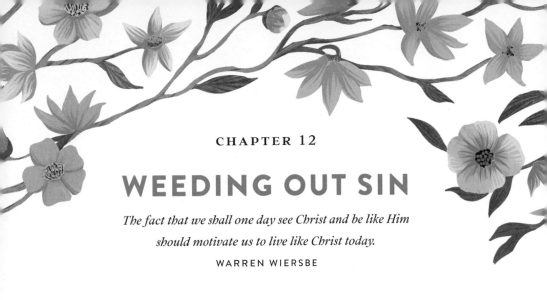

CHAPTER 12

WEEDING OUT SIN

The fact that we shall one day see Christ and be like Him
should motivate us to live like Christ today.

WARREN WIERSBE

The Story of a Thirsty Woman

Hungry to know God's Word and obey it, she set out to live with intention and perfection. *Today,* she thought, *will be the day I obey Jesus fully and get it right.* By midmorning, she'd already gossiped about a coworker, complained about her commute, and let her fear prevent her from sharing her faith. She felt like a total failure, just as she had the day before. At lunch, she shared about her downhill day with a friend. Her friend responded with this timely reminder: "God's grace is greater than your bad attitude. It's greater than any mistake you've made. He doesn't require you to clean yourself up before you come to the throne of grace. He bends down and meets you right where you are. As you seek him, he will continue to weed out sin so you can become more like him every day. Mind the Gap of where you are and where you will be, trusting him every step of the way." In other words, her journey isn't over yet, because Jesus is always at work.

WHEN I WAS A LITTLE GIRL, if you'd asked me what I wanted to be when I grew up, the answer would have been different depending on the day. The long list of careers I wanted to pursue included (in no particular order) garbage collector, maid, Sonic waitress, fashion designer, overseas missionary, elementary school teacher, dolphin trainer, and, always, mother.

My current roles reflect this list, just in very different ways. I'm a collector of all the trash cans in our home, the sweeper of crumbs from the floor, the waitress to my family at mealtimes, the purchaser of my children's wardrobe, a missionary for Jesus where I am, and a trainer and teacher of these kiddos (who probably resemble little dolphins at times).

Where I am today is not where I thought I'd be. But perhaps even more significant, who I am today is not who I thought I'd be. Life rarely (if ever) follows our one-, five-, and ten-year plans. Over time, not only do our plans change, but *we* change.

You are not the same person today as you were when you were a kid or ten years ago—or even yesterday, for that matter.

You are constantly changing, and for the woman who is following Jesus, this is really good news.

WORKS IN PROGRESS

At the start of the day, I'll set out to be all I was meant to be, do everything I planned to do, and make an impact on those around me. And most of the time, when I get to the evening, I look back and wonder, *Where did the day go? How did I get so off track?* Which then leads me to a familiar cry of desperation: "Lord, how will you ever use this mess I've made?"

If I'm being completely honest, life as an adult isn't as exciting as I thought it would be. What I didn't realize in my naive youth was that "time brings change and change takes time."[1] Life isn't made up of only highlight reels or mountaintop moments; it also includes valleys, deserts, and long, monotonous walks between destinations. Even spiritual giants throughout history had their share of daily drudgery and soul sanctification.

The apostle Paul wrestled with his sinfulness: "Wretched man that I am! Who will deliver me from this body of death?" (Romans 7:24). In Paul's daily wrestling, he came to grasp the grace and salvation of Jesus Christ. Elisabeth Elliot, a missionary to Ecuador and a prolific author, also had her share of struggles. After her husband, Jim, was murdered, Elisabeth continued to do missionary work in Ecuador, sharing the gospel with the men who had killed her husband. Later, Elisabeth married a man named Addison Leitch, who was diagnosed with cancer and died just three and a half years after the wedding.[2]

Both the apostle Paul and Elisabeth Elliot were imperfect, work-in-progress human beings. They suffered and wondered and wrestled and struggled. But they lived for the only perfect human being who has ever lived: Jesus Christ. God used every trial and test they faced to show them his enduring faithfulness. We tend to focus on their mountaintop moments, but what brought them there were the long, grueling hikes upward.

Much of gardening work happens in the mundane, less-than-glamorous moments—weeding, cultivating, tending. In a similar way, our faith doesn't grow just in the big moments; it's tended daily in the small, often invisible acts of faithfulness and obedience. The point of being faithful is not to be placed on a pedestal but to magnify Christ, the perfect one. When we desire perfection for ourselves in order to be praised by others, we lose sight of knowing Jesus, who is perfect. But the more we seek to know Christ and delight in his perfection, the more we will be changed into his likeness. This doesn't happen overnight; it is a moment-by-moment, day-by-day process called sanctification.

I often wish God would hurry up his sanctification work so I would no longer have to deal with besetting sins and self-centered desires. But God doesn't work on my timetable, and he doesn't work in the way I think he should (see Isaiah 55:8-9). As long as we live on this earth, there will be a gap between the ideal and the real, the hoped for and the happening right now. There's a reason the self-help industry is a multibillion-dollar industry. As human beings, we are starkly aware of our brokenness, our fallenness, and our failure to measure up. We want to do whatever we can to bridge the gap and become the "best version of ourselves." And we want to get there as quickly and effortlessly as possible.

We've been wired to desire transformation. But where we veer off course is when we look for help, healing, and wholeness in the wrong places. We set yearly goals, hit the gym, and track our time in an effort to change, but we still feel stuck. We're not static human beings. Whether we're trying to or not, we change every day—for better or worse. By God's extravagant grace, we can change to be more like Jesus (see 2 Corinthians 3:18). This transformation doesn't happen quickly. It takes time; it takes every breath and the movement of the Holy Spirit in our hearts.

No matter how many days you live, you are a work in progress every one of them. As you seek Jesus in your daily life, he slowly but surely sanctifies your desires so you can reflect his image to the world around you. Someday the ragged garden plot of your life will be fully transformed, but that day won't happen until you breathe your last and enter glory. For now, the Well-Watered Woman embraces the sometimes painful process of sanctification, knowing it's the way to reflect the image of her Maker.

MIND THE GAP

On a trip to London many years ago, my mom and I were intrigued by the verbiage used in the public transportation system, specifically the phrase "Mind the Gap." This phrase was first introduced in London subways in 1968 to warn passengers of the gap they would step over when leaving the platform to board the train.[3] The phrase quickly gained popularity and is now used all over the world to caution passengers to watch their step.

The same is true in the life of the believer. The moment we're saved, we are sanctified. The word *sanctified* means "made holy" or "set apart." Sanctification is a basic Christian doctrine that should fill our hearts with faith, peace, and assurance. Apart from Jesus, we're dead in our sin, enemies of God, children of wrath (see Ephesians 2:1-3). Without Jesus' blood, there's nothing we can do to earn salvation, clean up our act, or become the "best version of ourselves." We become God's children not because of our merit but because of his mercy.

But sanctification is not a one-time event; it's a continual process of growing more like Jesus. There's a gap between who we are now and who we will become in Christ. The gap between where we are and where we want to be can be bridged only through the cross. No self-help book or program could ever do this. Through the Spirit's help, we are sanctified, and that's better than any self-help book.

Theologians identify two types of sanctification that are key to the Christian life: positional sanctification and progressive sanctification.

Positional Sanctification

Positional sanctification marks the believer's standing in Christ as holy, blameless, and righteous. In other words, when you follow Christ, confessing your sins and believing that God raised him from the dead, the blood of Jesus cleanses you from every past, present, and future sin (see Romans 10:9; 1 John 1:7). You are completely covered by Jesus' sacrifice on the cross! You are no longer dead in your sins; you are alive in Christ through the power of his resurrection from the dead (see Romans 6:8-11).

As a child of God, you are called, set apart, and made holy in his sight. "At the moment that they trust in Christ," Dr. W. Duncan Rankin explains, "new believers are called 'holy,' 'sanctified,' and 'saints' because they are different from the rest, united to Him by faith and by the Spirit."[4] Positional sanctification begins the moment you are saved by faith in Christ.

This has drastic implications for the well-watered life! It means you are free from the dominion of sin. You are free from your past failures, your present struggles, and your future stumbling. You are free from your inadequacy, free from your insecurity, and free from your insufficiency. You *are* free in Christ. This is a fact, an unmistakable truth.

However, living in the fullness of this freedom requires a day-by-day choice to embrace the reality of the work of the

Holy Spirit. You are made new, holy, and free in Christ, but each day the Spirit continues to sanctify you and reflect his image in your thoughts, actions, work, and relationships. This leads us to progressive sanctification.

Progressive Sanctification

Progressive sanctification is where "Minding the Gap" comes into the Christian life. This is the "already but not yet" aspect of faith. While you have already been made holy because Jesus' blood covers you, you are also called to strive after holiness, to embrace God's daily sanctification—to continually pull out the weeds that crowd out the good fruit in your soul (see Hebrews 12:14).

You are holy in Christ, but you are also *becoming* holy as you pursue a God-honoring, obedient, joyful life. Renowned spiritual formation teacher Dallas Willard is said to have put it this way: "The most important thing in your life is not what you do; it's who you become. That's what you will take into eternity." The goal of the Christian—the aim of the Well-Watered Woman—is to become more and more like Jesus every moment of every day.

This side of eternity, you won't live life perfectly. Ever. But you know the perfect one, and you can strive for holiness through his grace and enabling. Take a deep breath, and let that truth sink in.

Holiness is a position for the believer, but it's also a daily pursuit. You will be pulling weeds until the day you meet Jesus.

Learning to welcome the process of sanctification and to "Mind the Gap" between where you are and where God is taking you will lead to joy in every season.

HAPPINESS OR HOLINESS?

In his book *The Pursuit of Holiness*, Jerry Bridges describes sanctification as walking "in obedience—not victory."[5] This punched me in the gut when I first read it. God calls us first and foremost to obedience to his Word. We tend to focus so much on the victory and mastery of our sins and shortcomings that we miss our Savior in it all. Our focus on victory becomes self-centered rather than Christ focused. We want perfection over the perfect one.

I'm guilty of this through and through. Even as a little girl, I remember wanting to please everyone and be perfect in other people's eyes. If I messed up even in the least, I spiraled into frustration and determined never to let it happen again. I am now in my third decade of life, and the raging desire to not mess up still wages war in my soul, distracting my focus from God. But he uses all things, even my mistakes, to make me more like him. As he reveals my sinful nature and turns my heart toward him, I discover true happiness. To be happy is ultimately to be made holy in the sight of God.

Culture tells us to pursue happiness, and religion tells us to pursue holiness, but Christ tells us to pursue both because both are ultimately found in him. The way of Christ is the way of peace and happiness. True happiness is found in God alone, and holiness is made possible through Jesus' sacrifice on our behalf.

You don't have to choose between holiness and happiness. Living a holy, set-apart life doesn't mean you'll miss out on the fun things of this world and never be happy. As a matter of fact, it's the exact opposite! It means you'll be set free from shallow, fleeting happiness because the foundation of your happiness will be in God, the ultimate source of happiness! Pursuing holiness is pursuing happiness, and pursuing happiness is ultimately pursuing holiness. The cross is the bridge between your sinfulness and God's holiness, and it's the means to true happiness.

SLOW TO BLOOM

When my sons were four and one, my husband and I lost our third child. I never knew a miscarriage could hurt so much—physically, spiritually, and emotionally. Two days after celebrating Thanksgiving with my in-laws, I felt a shift in my body, and fear struck a dark note in my heart. I started bleeding, and deep down, I knew I was losing the baby.

In just a few days we would be home, and I had an appointment scheduled for our first ultrasound. As cramps invaded my body and the bleeding continued, my pregnancy nausea disappeared. By the time I made it to the doctor's appointment that Tuesday, the ultrasound showed an empty womb.

The loss was excruciating as my body underwent deeper pains than I knew possible. The grief felt unbearable at times yet also numbing. I went from being excited about this third baby to being shocked by the unexpected miscarriage. At first I was apprehensive about sharing the painful loss we were experiencing, but I also knew that I couldn't (and shouldn't) walk through it alone. I texted a few friends and mentors to pray alongside our family, and they immediately began caring for us in meaningful and tangible ways.

When I eventually shared our loss publicly, God opened my eyes to the number of people who had walked a similar path. Friends wrote encouraging messages that brought tears to my eyes, and many of them provided meals or sent thoughtful gifts to remember our third baby. One specific provision served as a powerful reminder of our friends' care—and the ongoing process of sanctification.

When I first received the package from two caring sisters in Christ, I was surprised to find a pot, a soil disc, and an amaryllis flower bulb inside. I was excited about the idea of growing an amaryllis, but I was also afraid I would fail. I already felt as if my body had failed me in growing and sustaining our child, and I couldn't bear the thought of trying to grow a flower and not being successful at that, either. Though the doctor had assured me that the miscarriage wasn't caused by my body failing, I was still afraid of not being able to nurture life again.

Despite my fear, I planted the flower because I wanted to

honor the gift. For weeks the plant looked the same. I didn't even want to share a picture of this measly shoot with the friends who had given it to me.

In his letter to the church at Corinth, the apostle Paul described the process of progressive sanctification: "We all, with unveiled face, beholding the glory of the Lord, are being transformed into the same image from one degree of glory to another. For this comes from the Lord who is the Spirit" (2 Corinthians 3:18). Beholding Christ means adoring him and being sanctified by the Holy Spirit as we become more aware of our sinfulness and his perfection. Beholding takes time, intention, and focus. But the more we behold the glory of God in the Word and in Christ, the more we are transformed. This, in turn, leads to greater joy and rejoicing in the one who pardons our sin.

After about six weeks, I noticed that my little amaryllis plant seemed to grow a few inches overnight. It went from being an inch tall to four inches tall, then eight inches, then twelve. Now it was a whopping thirty-two inches tall and beginning to bloom—slowly but surely. Each day I stared at the tip that reached upward, hoping to see some color, aching to see the flowers burst from their buds. This plant was becoming what it was meant to be. There's a gap between this plant as a bulb and this plant at full bloom. You can't skip any of the steps along the way—every part of the process is necessary. So it is with our own journey of sanctification.

My friend Ruth Chou Simons often says, "We don't have to be blooming to be growing," and I couldn't think of a better way to describe the process of sanctification.[6] My amaryllis, even when it isn't in full bloom, is a daily reminder that God is doing a work in my heart and mind, growing me and transforming me to become more like Jesus. He uses everything to achieve this goal—the person who cuts me off when I'm driving, my child who is insistent on eating cookies before dinner, my own laziness, the hurt of a friend, the daily struggle of desiring my phone too much. All these drive me to the Cross for grace, mercy, and help. They expose my sinful tendencies and show me how Christ would live, respond, and act. They lead to slow, steady growth.

These invisible steps are necessary to get to the end result. There's a gap between where you are and where you will someday be. Embrace the process of becoming like Christ. You are both sanctified and being sanctified at the same time. The amaryllis bulb was still an amaryllis even before it bloomed.

OBSESS OVER HIS FAITHFULNESS, NOT YOUR FAILURES

The more we become aware of God's holiness, the more we are aware of how far we are from holiness ourselves. I love how Jerry Bridges describes it: "As we grow in the *knowledge* of God's holiness, even though we are also growing in the *practice* of holiness it seems the gap between our knowledge and our practice always gets wider. This is the Holy Spirit's way of drawing us to more and more holiness."[7] Obsessing over failure is ultimately self-centered and only leads us back into a spiral of disappointment. In the pursuit of holiness and happiness in God, we should instead obsess over his faithfulness.

He is faithful, even when we fail (see 2 Timothy 2:13).

He is faithful yesterday, today, and forever (see Hebrews 13:8).

Obsess over his faithfulness, not your failures.

Let every failure be a reminder to "Mind the Gap," acknowledging that you are a work in progress and that every fruitful garden has weeds to be pulled. The more aware you are of your sin, the more you will embrace the grace of God and turn toward a life of holiness.

When you plant and don't see a harvest right away, don't be afraid that victory won't come. Simply be obedient to tend your garden and trust God with the growth.

END OF CONSTRUCTION

The epitaph Ruth Bell Graham requested for her gravestone is a witty reminder to every onlooker: "End of Construction— Thank you for your patience."[8] Ruth, wife of well-known evangelist Billy Graham, knew what it meant to "Mind the Gap" as she followed Jesus and became more like him. She was well aware of her frailty as a human and obsessed over his faithfulness, despite her failures.

After driving past a road sign one day that signaled to

passing cars that the construction zone was ending, she asked her family to have this statement etched on her gravestone as a reminder that her life had been a work in progress. It was all for Jesus and all because of Jesus.

Someday our own soul construction will come to an end. The question is, What will you do in the meantime? Will you pursue a holy life that pleases God and shows the world around you that he is real and he is worth it?

Thanks to the patience of the Gardener, the Well-Watered Woman is always growing in grace.

THE WELL-WATERED WOMAN
EMBRACES SANCTIFICATION,
KNOWING IT'S THE ONLY PATH
TO FLOURISHING.

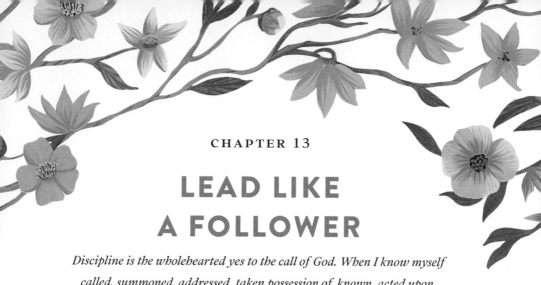

CHAPTER 13

LEAD LIKE
A FOLLOWER

Discipline is the wholehearted yes to the call of God. When I know myself
called, summoned, addressed, taken possession of, known, acted upon,
I have heard the Master. I put myself gladly, fully, and forever
at His disposal, and to whatever He says my answer is yes.
ELISABETH ELLIOT

The Story of a Thirsty Woman

She looked around to see what everyone else was doing and
decided to follow suit. She desperately wanted to lead those
around her, but the way she led looked more like conforming.
She spent countless hours trying to make sure she was following the latest trends and styles, and it left her feeling hollow
and exhausted. She had neglected the most important thing—
spending time with Jesus, learning his way of life. After years
of living on empty and chasing the latest craze, she had all but
forgotten who she was. She was on the cusp of discovering that

wholeheartedly following Jesus would make her look different, act different, think different, and feel different—and that was a good thing.

———————————

I USED TO TRY to be like everyone else. For as long as I can remember, there was always *someone* I looked up to, someone I wanted to shape my actions and appearances around. When I was twelve, I copied the Olsen twins, like most girls did in the nineties. I got my hair cut to mimic one of their short, flipped-out hair styles, and when I came home with my spunky new do, I asked my dad what he thought. His first words, which were clearly not thought through, were, "I like it! You look like a little Dutch girl!" I ditched that hairstyle pretty quickly.

In middle school I wanted to be popular, and I did my best to conform to my peers. There was a girl named Sarah I spent a lot of time with. She was popular and liked by everyone, but her choices didn't reflect the Word's standards. I knew Sarah for only a year, but that year had a profoundly negative impact on me at the time. She introduced me to words I knew I shouldn't say and movies I knew I shouldn't watch, and they stuck in my mind long after I left the school where we met.

When I was in high school, there was Rachel. She was beautiful—the best cheerleader, with long blonde hair and the most stylish outfits. I wanted to dress like her, act like her, and look like her. But as much as I tried, I never became just like her. I felt like an outcast a lot of the time, and deep down I thought I didn't measure up to the other girls around me. My first broken heart came when I found out the boy I was friends with and had a crush on was actually dating another girl. I couldn't seem to figure out what was wrong with me, and I expended a lot of effort trying to "fix" myself. I thought a lot about the missing pieces of my life, all while missing out on who God has always been and who he made me to be.

The struggle to be like others continued into my college and adult years. There's always someone else who seems to do life better—someone who is more gifted, more talented, more beautiful. Social media has only amplified this struggle. We compare our worst moments to other people's best ones. We try to make our ordinary days mirror what we see on a highlight reel, and it's never enough. All too quickly I can bookmark someone's "picture perfect" social media life and lose sight of where God has me.

As I've grown older, I've started to look for different qualities in the women I model my life after. I want to imitate women who pursue Jesus and the Word wholeheartedly—women whose beauty radiates from their character rather than the perfect haircut or the most beautifully designed living room. The best leaders are the best followers—the ones who move out of the way so Jesus can shine through. When the Cross is first in someone's life, the crowd takes notice. The

Well-Watered Woman looks to the Cross before the crowd and follows Christ wholeheartedly.

FOLLOWERS OF THE WAY

When I sought to follow other people, my life conformed to theirs, but when I started seeking to follow Christ, my life started conforming to his. Following Jesus isn't a matter of fitting in with the world; it's a matter of standing out. This is nothing new. Going back to the early church, we see the disciples learning what it meant to forsake the world to fully follow Christ. Some disciples lost their livelihoods, some lost their reputations, and some lost their lives (see Luke 9:57-62). They were persecuted, perplexed, cast down, and forsaken, yet they counted it all joy to stand up for Christ, who first stood up for them on the cross (see 2 Corinthians 4:7-12).

After Jesus was raised from the dead, conquering death and shattering the bondage of sin, he appeared before the disciples as well as more than "five hundred brothers," proclaiming the Kingdom of God and sending them out as ambassadors and witnesses of the gospel (1 Corinthians 15:3-10). The last words Jesus spoke before ascending into heaven summarize the commission of the apostles: "You will receive power when the Holy Spirit has come upon you, and you will be my witnesses in Jerusalem and in all Judea and Samaria, and to the ends of the earth" (Acts 1:8).

The disciples did just that. As the book of Acts unfolds, the apostle Luke, who compiled the narrative, methodically shows how they went to Jerusalem, Judea, and Samaria, and then to the ends of the earth, to share about the resurrection of Christ. The gospel had captured their hearts, and they lived like it was true.

Before these believers were called Christians, they were called followers of "the Way." In Acts 9:2, we read about the persecution of those "belonging to the Way." The word *Way* in this context refers back to Jesus, who called himself "the way, the truth, and the life" (John 14:6, NLT). The people who followed Jesus shaped their lives around his ways and his words. Jesus wasn't merely a man to imitate; he was their very life. Even in the face of persecution, their eyes were glued to their risen Savior, who had defeated death and continued to lead them in triumph. They didn't merely follow a set of rules; they followed the person of Jesus and led others straight to him.

Saul, a prominent Jewish leader at the time, committed his life to persecuting followers of the Way. One day while he was traveling, a light from heaven appeared before him. Falling to the ground, he heard a voice say, "Saul, Saul, why are you persecuting me?" (Acts 9:4). The voice of the one speaking to him was the very one he was persecuting—Jesus, the Way. Talk about a moment of reversal!

Saul (who later became known as Paul), the murderer and threat bringer, turned from his past ways to follow *the* Way. He immediately went out to preach and proclaim the gospel that had wrecked and rebuilt his life. The persecutor became the persecuted preacher. The man who once incited people toward violence now led people to the victor, Jesus.

The start of Paul's journey to becoming a follower of the Way proves that God can use absolutely anyone to make his name great. He calls the broken down and the busted up—all those who seem like least likely candidates—to believe in him and proclaim his Kingdom. Jesus isn't limited by our past or our former sins. He's able to redeem, restore, and renew anyone who receives him—even a man like Paul.

FOLLOW ME AS I FOLLOW CHRIST

We live in a world obsessed with followers. With the rise of social media, the concept of "follower" has all but lost its meaning. Simply clicking "like" or "follow" has become the definition of friendship, interest, and commitment, and it reflects the way many people follow Jesus.

When I first joined social media, I was immediately drawn to the lure of followers. I began to base my identity on numbers—I started to buy into the idea that my reach determined my worthiness. If my follower count went down, I'd get discouraged, overanalyzing what I'd posted. I allowed likes, comments, and follows to dictate how I felt and what I shared. In a sense, I put myself in "Instagram jail," and it kept me from living fully and freely for Christ. This must be one of the ugliest parts of human nature—how self-focused we can become without even realizing it.

Social media says, "Follow me!" Christians, on the other hand, say, "Follow me as I follow Christ." Ultimately, a follower count means absolutely nothing if we're not leading people to Jesus. Every number represents a person, and every person has been created in the image of God. Something I've been trying to ask myself regularly is, *Where am I leading people? To the Cross? Or to the never-satisfied crowd?*

It pains me to see girls spending the majority of their days with phones in hand, taking selfies and creating highlight reels while they're crumbling on the inside. They're searching endlessly, wondering where true contentment can be found. Whether we realize it or not, social media shapes the way we think, the way we spend our time, the way we act, and the way we live. Not only are we shaped by it, but we are also shaping others with what we post and share. Ultimately, we share out of the overflow of our hearts—we share what we treasure most (see Luke 6:45).

Paul, the unlikely convert to Christianity, immediately began to share about Jesus. He became the most prolific writer of the New Testament, and through his testimony, more and more people became followers of the Way. In his letter to the church at Corinth, Paul made this bold statement: "Follow my example as I follow the example of Christ" (1 Corinthians 11:1, NIV). Paul knew that people are quick to imitate the lives of others. He redeems this notion of imitation by encouraging us to be imitators of Christ, the only one worth imitating and following.

To imitate those who imitate Christ is to seek the glory of God, to follow the Way, and to show the world that this Jesus we proclaim isn't just worthy of our words; he is worthy of our lives.

ARE YOU LEADING LIKE A FOLLOWER?

You are both a follower *and* a leader. No matter who you are, someone is taking note of your actions, your speech, your decisions, and your lifestyle. People are watching the way you handle daily struggles, the way you walk through hardship, the way you interact with others. Which way are you leading them? Are you leading like a wholehearted follower of the Way? Or are you leading like a follower of the world?

In the same vein, who are you following? Who is shaping your life? Are the people you look up to, both past and present, people who lead you to Jesus? Don't underestimate the power of the media you take in, the words you read, the shows you watch, and the people you follow. The ripple effect can impact generations to come.

Refuse to buy the lie that your past hinders you from following Jesus in the present. Paul wasn't proud of his past, but he used it as an opportunity to share the power of the gospel. If he had allowed his past failures to define him, he never would have shared the gospel. He would have kept quiet and remained undercover. But he didn't. He grasped the fullness of the gospel and he couldn't keep quiet about it, so he shared loudly, boldly, and fearlessly. Eventually it led to his death (see Philippians 1:21). He went from being a world follower to a Way follower, and his faithfulness continues to lead people around the world to salvation in Christ.

A life that's well lived and well watered is a life that follows Jesus and leads others to him.

LEAD FROM THE OVERFLOW, NOT THE UNDERTOW

Francis Chan tells of a Christian leader who said, "I refuse to let my public passion exceed my private devotion."[1] This is the secret to leading like a follower. Outward appearances mean nothing when our hearts aren't first set on Christ. In a world that says, "Follow the crowd," we say, "Follow Christ!" Instead of putting on the appearance of Christianity, we put on Christ as we lead a life of private devotion that, in turn, affects the overflow of everything we say, do, and post.

When my husband and I were dating, I drove a beat-up, barely functioning Ford Taurus. This little gray vehicle had already been through several drivers before it came into my possession, and it constantly gave me trouble. Seeing that the car was having issues, Greg offered to take it to a mechanic. I willingly accepted the offer, having successfully avoided a car repair shop up to that point. The next day he came to me bearing good news and bad news. The good news: my car would be spared impending death for a time and was up and running again. The bad news: I had driven my rickety vehicle ten thousand miles past its routine oil change.

Ten. *Thousand.* Miles.

The engine was burning up, and the car was on its last legs. The mechanic asked why I hadn't taken it in when the check engine light came on. Well, that was an easy answer. I had placed a notecard with a Bible verse written on it on the dashboard so I could work on memorizing it. I never saw the flashing light, and I drove my car until it was almost beyond repair . . . ten thousand miles past its need for upkeep. The car worked, barely, but there were issues that could have been avoided if I'd paid more attention.

The same thing happens in our walk with Christ when we focus on outward affection over private devotion. We lead, pour out, and keep pressing on while neglecting regular soul maintenance. We live our lives *for* Jesus while missing out on intimacy *with* him. Busyness, productivity, achievement, and distraction become our driving forces, covering up the flashing light that says, "Slow down! Be still! Bring your soul in for maintenance so you can keep leading others to Jesus." Leading on empty only results in burnout. But Jesus invites us to a better life.

PUT "HE" BEFORE "SHE"

Trying to be like everyone else will exhaust you, drain you, and dry you up. This kind of following will cause you to lose sight of the unique way God created you and the purposes he has designed for you. No matter what stage of life you're in, the temptation to be like everyone else will always be there. There will always be a "she" you want to imitate. But when you put "he" before "she," your entire perspective changes.

God didn't make a mistake when he made you. He doesn't want you to just be like her; he wants you to be like Jesus. Instead of trying to be like someone else, embrace who God made you to be and run hard after Jesus. Cheer on your sisters in their missions and races, but keep your eyes on the prize of knowing Christ and making him known. Lead like a follower, and leave your "following" up to him.

THE WELL-WATERED WOMAN

FOLLOWS JESUS

WHOLEHEARTEDLY,

KNOWING THAT IN ORDER

TO LEAD WELL,

SHE MUST FIRST BE

A DISCIPLE OF JESUS.

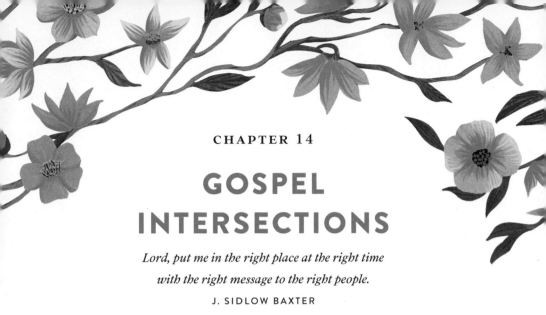

CHAPTER 14

GOSPEL INTERSECTIONS

Lord, put me in the right place at the right time
with the right message to the right people.

J. SIDLOW BAXTER

The Story of a Thirsty Woman

She stood in line at the grocery store, phone in hand, scrolling the latest headlines and tapping her foot. When it was almost her turn, she set her phone down to start moving her items onto the conveyer belt. She paused when she caught the eye of the woman slowly loading her cart in front of her and noticed the profound sadness in her gaze. Her heart was stirred with conviction and compassion, and she began asking simple questions to learn the woman's story. After they both checked out, they continued to chat on their way to the parking lot. By the end of the conversation, she'd learned that the woman had recently lost her father in a car accident and was barely making it through each day. She offered to pray for her, and soon the woman was smiling again. She wondered how many times she missed the hand of God intersecting her everyday life, simply because her mind was occupied with other things. She drove home, reminded that gospel intersections are everywhere—she just needed to look up, be available, and trust God to move.

THE FIRST TIME I met Karen Alexander Doyel, I knew there was something different about her. We were both attending meetings for women's ministry leaders hosted in Nashville, and our initial encounter was not by accident. What drew me to her wasn't her appearance; it was her confidence, her calm demeanor, her character. There wasn't anything special or unique about the way she looked. As a matter of fact, on the outside, she was quite small and frail looking. But there was an exuberant strength in her words and presence, as if she'd fought a battle and still bore the scars of victory. I knew right away that I wanted to have what she had.

In that first brief conversation, we discovered we lived about twenty minutes from each other in Knoxville, Tennessee. My husband and I had moved there recently, and I'd been praying for a mentor to walk alongside me during those early months of marriage and ministry.

When I got home from the event, I sent Karen an e-mail,

asking if she'd be willing to meet with me. Even if we just had one conversation, I wanted to glean as much wisdom from her as possible. She quickly responded that she would love to get together at her house. "I'm excited to spend time with you, and I know we'll learn from each other!" she said. Karen's humble and gentle spirit even illuminated the words in her e-mail.

As we sat together in her living room, I learned that she did have many scars—on both her soul and her body. At the time we met, she had ovarian cancer. But this wasn't the only fiery furnace she'd endured.

Years prior, her husband, Doug, had died in a tragic accident while camping with his three sons on the eve of Y2K. After deciding on a whim to go on a year-end adventure, Doug and the boys packed their bags and hiked up a mountain in the dark. When they reached the top, they pulled out their camping gear, stoked a fire, and gazed in awe at the twinkling stars above.

Doug stood from his camping chair, looked up at the heavens, and said with reverence, "What an amazing God we have to have created such beauty, I can't imagine anyone seeing this and not believing in the Creator."[1] The next thing the boys heard was his chair rattling—and then he was gone, falling down the side of the cliff.

Back at home in those early morning hours, when her sons were desperately trying to find their father, Karen was awake, burdened to pray for her boys, John, Stephen, and Mark. There was no way she could have known that two of her sons had jumped over the cliff edge in an attempt to find their father, not realizing there was a two-hundred-foot free fall below.

Mark was holding on to the side of the cliff, and Stephen caught hold of a small tree branch on the side of the mountain. Reciting the Lord's Prayer for strength and peace, Stephen painstakingly climbed back up to the top of the cliff, confident that angels were protecting him from falling. Mark found his way back to the top as well. By God's grace, Karen's boys didn't fall to the bottom of the mountain. But her husband, the love of her life, was already in the presence of Jesus.

Gripping my cup of coffee, I leaned in closer, holding my breath as she shared her testimony of God's faithfulness. My eyes were full of tears, and my heart was racing. Suddenly, my cup of coffee didn't matter anymore, much less the petty worries of the day before. As I listened to Karen talk about God's redemption and healing after the heartbreaking loss of her husband, my soul was shaken from its slumber. I didn't want to endure the kind of loss Karen had gone through, but I longed to experience the nearness of eternity she felt every day.

Karen's story of heartache and hope stirred in me an urgency to live for Christ alone, taking advantage of every opportunity to share about him. The same strength I saw in her the first time we met spilled out even as she shared about her loss. Despite the hardships she faced, she still had joy and confidence in God, her Sustainer, and she radiated the glory and goodness of God.

We continued to meet together in the coming weeks to talk

about the Word while sipping coffee or tea in her living room. The drinks never stayed hot. The moment we sat down, we started talking fervently and forgot all about our beverages. Our times together were full of passion for the Word, but they were rarely without interruption. Karen delighted when our meeting time coincided with visits from her home nurses, who would come to administer antibodies to boost her immune system. She loved that the nurses would hear about her God, who remained faithful through the dark nights of the soul.

Karen had once traveled all over the world, speaking at women's gatherings and sharing the Good News of Christ. When her sickness kept her homebound, she continued ministering to those around her, even the home nurses.[2]

OUR BETTER STORY

The year before she died from her final battle with cancer, I asked Karen if I could record her testimony over the phone. She agreed, but instead of going into the details of her losses, she boasted about God's faithfulness. She was consumed with Christ. She could have been consumed with all that had gone wrong in her life—the death of her husband, her son's cancer diagnosis, and her own battles with cancer. She could have complained that she'd been dealt a bad hand and was suffering unfairly. Instead, she *rejoiced*. She *praised*. She *worshiped*. She wanted people to know that through it all, Jesus held her together, and she couldn't wait to see him face-to-face.

Karen is forever a picture to me of the Well-Watered Woman. She wasn't perfect, and her story wasn't a fairy tale—from a human perspective, at least. But her days held eternal worth, and her impact still reaches people around the world.

I'm sure your story is also messy and imperfect. No doubt you've experienced your own pains and heartbreaks. And yet one truth remains: Jesus is our true and better story. The gospel intersects with every aspect of our lives, bringing joy in the sorrow, hope in the mourning, and peace in the turmoil. Your story is an opportunity to experience the gospel, preach the gospel, and live out the gospel right where you are. The gospel-saturated life begins with the ministry of faithfulness in the little things.

FAITHFULNESS IN THE LITTLE THINGS

"If this is what it means to follow Jesus, I don't know if I can do it," I told Karen over the phone about two years after we started meeting together. Just as doors were opening in my ministry to share Christ with others, the darkness of depression was overshadowing my soul. It felt like the closer I got to Jesus, the more spiritual warfare I experienced. If following Jesus meant life was going to be this hard, I wasn't sure I could do it. Ministry felt like a frontline battle, and I was tired of fighting in my own strength.

"You've got to put on your armor and fight, Gretchen!" Karen urged. "The enemy does *not* want you to share Christ, but Jesus is greater. Speak the Word out loud. March around your house declaring it. The enemy has to flee at the name of Jesus. I'm fighting for you on my end. We have to go to battle, sister!" Karen's words broke into my weary soul and shone a flashlight of hope in the darkness.

Karen taught me that true ministry is not about ease or abundance; it's about faithfulness and obedience. In Paul's letter to the church at Corinth, he offered similar encouragement:

> Therefore, having this ministry by the mercy of God, we do not lose heart. But we have renounced disgraceful, underhanded ways. We refuse to practice cunning or to tamper with God's word, but by the open statement of the truth we would commend ourselves to everyone's conscience in the sight of God. . . . For what we proclaim is not ourselves, but Jesus Christ as Lord, with ourselves as your servants for Jesus' sake.
>
> 2 CORINTHIANS 4:1-2, 5

For the believer, proclaiming the gospel isn't just a suggestion; it's a command. True ministry isn't just done on a platform or on a stage in front a crowd. It's done in your home when you sit with your toddler and explain the goodness of God. It's done when you pause to talk to a stranger and share the love of Christ. It is done when you lay down your desire to be praised, and you fold laundry out of a love for God. True ministry is faithfulness in the little things (see Luke 16:10). It begins with a heart focused squarely on Christ Jesus, who modeled a life of ministry and faithfulness himself.

MINISTRY AT YOUR FEET

Jesus walked on earth for a total of thirty-three years, but only a handful of them are recorded in Scripture. His birth is detailed in the Gospels as the miraculous fulfillment of long-awaited prophecies, and his final years are captured in detail, but the bulk of his life is unrecorded.

Here's what we do know about the thirty unrecorded years of Jesus' life: he was tempted in every way yet was without sin, he was faithful to the Father in everything, and he lived what he came to preach (see Hebrews 4:15). Like his earthly father, Joseph, Jesus was a craftsman.[3] Jesus labored physically, working with his hands and building with materials he'd made at the dawn of time (see John 1:1; Genesis 1:1).

In his three years of recorded ministry, Jesus faithfully ministered to the people who were right at his feet. When he walked through crowds, he paid attention to those who were around him, listening to the voices calling to him and noting the hands of those touching him. He was interrupted from spending time alone with the Father by the needy, impatient disciples (see Mark 1:35-37). He welcomed children into his lap, delighting in their presence and teaching adults to imitate their childlike faith (see Matthew 18:3-4; 19:13-15). Jesus ministered to those who crossed his path, showing us what this looks like through his own example.

Before facing the Cross, Jesus spent time with his disciples, teaching them, preparing them, and praying for them. Jesus lived knowing he would die. He lived with the Cross always before him and the world behind him, and he fiercely loved those who were his.

John records this example of Jesus' sacrificial love:

> Jesus, knowing that the Father had given all things into his hands, and that he had come from God and was going back to God, rose from supper. He laid aside his outer garments, and taking a towel, tied it around his waist. Then he poured water into a basin and began to wash the disciples' feet and to wipe them with the towel that was wrapped around him.
> JOHN 13:3-5

During Jesus' day, foot washing was a task reserved for the lowliest of non-Jewish servants. People wore sandals and walked along dusty roads all day, and their feet were a far cry from clean. As always, Jesus flipped cultural standards upside down and showed the disciples—and us—what it means to serve and to love. Knowing he was going to die, he cleansed their feet as a picture of their ultimate soul cleansing.[4] Jesus even washed the feet of Judas Iscariot, who would ultimately betray him. He showed us that the way of the Kingdom is the way of bending down low and serving at every opportunity.

John continues describing this event:

> When he had washed their feet and put on his outer garments and resumed his place, he said to them, "Do you understand what I have done to you? You call me Teacher and Lord, and you are right, for so I am. If I then, your Lord and Teacher, have washed your feet, you also ought to wash one another's feet. For I have given you an example, that you also should do just as I have done to you."
>
> JOHN 13:12-15

Gospel intersections are all around us. There are always opportunities to bend low and wash one another's feet through humble service and sacrifice.

Elisabeth Elliot wrote this honest prayer that depicts the life of a humble foot washer: "Lord, break the chains that hold me to myself; free me to be Your happy slave—that is, to be the happy foot washer of anyone today who needs his feet washed, his supper cooked, his faults overlooked, his work commended, his failure forgiven, his griefs consoled or his button sewed on. Let me not imagine that my love for You is very great if I am unwilling to do for a human being something very small."[5] Great love for God is revealed in our willingness to do small things for him, to serve those in front of us, and to bend low to wash another's feet.

Being a humble foot washer is the privilege of the Well-Watered Woman. Christ-centered service points to the one we serve and follow. It sets us apart in a world where we feel pressure to elevate ourselves and see how others can benefit us.

THE MINISTRY OF EYE CONTACT

Karen once told me that she made a point of not talking on her phone when she was at the grocery store. She thought of everything, even going to the store, as an opportunity to be a vessel for Christ, to pray for others, to look people in the eye, and to give them the dignity they deserve. In an age of distraction, eye contact is no longer the norm. People walk around with their heads down, tapping away at their phones, or with earbuds in place, oblivious to those around them. We even continue our phone conversations in the checkout line, forgetting that there's a real person standing in front of us to show love to, talk to, and give our full attention to. It makes me wonder how many opportunities I miss out on each day by having my eyes glued to my digital devices.

When I was in college, before cell phones recorded every waking moment of our day, a few of my friends and I would go onto campus and pray for opportunities to share our faith. We would walk through the dining areas, study lounges, and busy hallways praying for people we saw and starting conversations when we felt led to. Our encounters weren't always monumental, but God gave us some amazing opportunities to share the gospel, pray for the hurting, and extend the love of Jesus to people in need.

It's been more than a decade since those days, and my life has changed a lot in the meantime. I've moved several times, and I'm now married and have two children. But even though life has changed, the gospel hasn't—and neither have opportunities to share it. I have to wonder, *What kind of revival would happen if I put down my phone and instead went on a walk to pray for my neighbors? What if instead of watching TV or browsing the internet during my free time, I went out of my way to encourage someone?* Jesus modeled for us the ministry of eye contact and presence. He showed us that it's possible to make every moment count.

When Jesus taught people and spent time with them, he looked at them and gave them his full presence and attention. He wasn't distracted with "more important" things. And with one look into his eyes, a person's life could be changed forever.

DO YOU REALLY SEE?

Luke records a powerful moment when a sinful woman was forgiven by Jesus (see Luke 7:36-50). But this story isn't just about the forgiveness of the woman's sins; it's also about the power of seeing those around us.

In this story, Jesus was dining with a Pharisee. While he was reclining, a "woman of the city, who was a sinner" came to the Pharisee's house and brought her expensive alabaster flask of ointment to pour on Jesus' feet (Luke 7:37). Weeping, the woman wiped his feet with her hair and kissed them. The Pharisee was appalled by the woman's display and Jesus' receptiveness to her gift. He said to himself, "If this man were a prophet, he would have known who and what sort of woman this is who is touching him, for she is a sinner" (verse 39).

Jesus responded right away to Simon, the prideful and blinded Pharisee, who had missed the point of the moment.

> Turning toward the woman he said to Simon, *"Do you see this woman?* I entered your house; you gave me no water for my feet, but she has wet my feet with her tears and wiped them with her hair. . . . You did not anoint my head with oil, but she has anointed my feet with ointment. Therefore I tell you, her sins, which are many, are forgiven—for she loved much. But he who is forgiven little, loves little."
>
> LUKE 7:44-47 (EMPHASIS ADDED)

Jesus asked Simon, "Do you see this woman?" Though the woman was in Simon's presence, he didn't really see her the way Jesus did. In his arrogance, he was preoccupied, and he missed the opportunity to see deeper—past her appearance, down to her heart. But Jesus saw her, and he opened Simon's eyes to see her too.

Jesus' challenge to Simon is the same as the challenge to us. Do you see?

Do you see those around you who are broken, beaten, and bruised?

Do you see those in need of love, grace, and mercy?

Do you see the hungry and homeless?

Do you see the widow and the orphan?

Do you see your neighbor?

Jesus taught us that the ministry of eye contact and the ministry of presence can powerfully change the person being seen . . . *and* the one seeing.

IN HIS IMAGE

The Well-Watered Woman sees everyone around her as created in the image of God, or *imago Dei*. Differences such as age, ethnicity, class, profession, and culture fall to the wayside when you begin seeing people as God's unique, intricate creations and not mere accidents. The person in the checkout line who may be completely different from you—in demeanor, appearance, and speech—was made by the same God (see Genesis 1:27).

I believe with all my heart that our days would be radically different if we began walking into stores, malls, classrooms, cubicles, and airports with the perspective that every person around us is made in God's image. There are people to be loved, seen, and noticed. There is ministry to be fulfilled right at your feet—with your kids, your students, your coworkers, your friends, your family, and even strangers. There are "foot washing" opportunities all around you that may look like offering a helping hand with someone's groceries or praying on the spot for a sister in Christ or preparing a homemade meal for a family going through a hard time.

You are a minister of the gospel, an agent of truth, a vehicle of blessing. Don't keep the gospel to yourself. Share it freely, faithfully, and fully, just as it was given to you through Christ.

GOSPEL INTERSECTIONS AT A FUNERAL

In her last days on earth, Karen wrote a letter to her sons with the intent that it be read at her funeral. She knew her time was limited, and she wanted her remaining hours and final words to leave a lasting legacy. She lived her life for the glory of God and made the most of every gospel intersection, even at the end. Here's a snapshot of what she poured out in that letter:

> *As I sit here tonight, I have so much to be grateful for. I could name my blessings for the rest of the night. I feel that for some unknown reason our God looked at me and said, "I really love that girl, I am going to bless her socks off!" And He has!*
>
> *Each trial has been felt as special attention from my Father in Heaven. He ordained difficult circumstances just so He and I could spend time together. He has held me in His arms more times than I can count. He has listened to my heart break and*

tenderly mended it back stronger than ever. My Father has let my tears drop on Him and has held them as though they were treasures. How can I explain such an incredible love? How can I tell you the joy that I have because of the sweet way our God has entered into my life and taken over?

If I would have known in advance, I am sure I would have had suggestions for Him. I can hear me telling Him that I cannot do it, I don't want to do it or even that I refuse to do it! I certainly would have been fearful as my trust and faith in Him had to grow through each difficult time.

The most incredible gift has been my Jesus and His forgiveness. Oh family, what a mess up I have been. I have made some horrible mistakes. Some you have seen. Some have affected you, some I pray you will never know about. The thing is . . . I am completely, totally forgiven! Can you believe it? It is so amazing that I am covered, righteous, blameless and unconditionally loved by the God who made the Heavens and the earth!!! How can I express my gratitude? What words can express the fullness of joy, happiness, peace that comes with the blood of our precious Jesus. Forgiven and allowed to serve our Risen Lord—it is difficult to fathom, but it is true—He is real, alive and everything to me! When I speak of Him, my heart races, my energy rises, my entire physical being seems to sing. . . . Teaching His Word, speaking His Name, what an honor and thrill. I could go on if I had the words, but you get the point, don't you?[6]

Karen was a Well-Watered Woman. She took every opportunity to share Jesus—at the grocery store, at chemo treatments, with her grandkids, and even at her own funeral. The legacy she left was not because of her own goodness or perfection but because of God's goodness at work within and through her. Gospel intersections are everywhere, and we'll see them if we look with the eyes of Jesus.

THE WELL-WATERED WOMAN

LOOKS FOR GOSPEL INTERSECTIONS

IN HER EVERYDAY LIFE,

KNOWING THAT EVEN

THE MUNDANE MATTERS

IN THE KINGDOM OF GOD.

CHAPTER 15

YOUR MISSION IS NOW

The place between your own two feet at any time—
that is your mission field.

JILL BRISCOE

The Story of a Thirsty Woman

She wished God would just tell her what to do next. *Why does it have to be so hard to figure out what his will is?* she wondered. She felt like she was constantly trying to connect the dots to figure out what her life should be. She didn't know what to eat for lunch, let alone what to do with her life or who to marry. She stood at a crossroads, looking to the right and to the left, paralyzed with fear. What if she took the wrong route? What if she missed her purpose? If only life came with a road map, everything would be easier. She wished there were a message written in the sky or an arrow sketched on the sidewalk. What she didn't realize was that the answer was right there in the Word: Jesus simply said, "Follow me." She didn't need to know every step; she just needed to follow the one who held the map.

IT WAS A CLOUDY MORNING in Washington State as we began our journey north to Mount Rainier. We were hopeful the clouds would clear at some point, but we were determined to have an adventure—whether under cloudy or clear skies. My brother moved to Seattle a number of years ago, and it's always a treat to visit him and his family and explore the West Coast.

On this particular trip, we packed our hiking boots so we could trek up one of the Paradise trails and enjoy the view. Portions of Mount Rainier can be hiked by the average person only during the brief summer months when the snow melts and the paths are clear. The timing of our vacation was right, so we went for it.

My husband, the planner of our adventures, opted for what was cited on the park map as one of the most strenuous hikes, assuring us that it was "only" five and a half miles. What we didn't know was that the majority of those five and a half miles were over rugged uphill terrain. About halfway up our initial ascent, I quickly regretted agreeing to this. Considering my brother's long legs and my husband's stamina, I wasn't sure I could keep up or if I'd survive the trek back down. The only thing that kept me going was the promise of wildflowers along the way and the thought of ice cream after the hike. (If you want to get me to do something hard in life, just promise me flowers and good food in the end, and I'm game.)

Up we went for hours and hours. The clouds eventually cleared, despite the weather app's forecast, and we could see for miles—winding rivers, twisting trails, deep crevices, lush evergreens. We stopped several times to catch our breath but also to catch the sights. The flowers were scarce on the front end of the hike, and I was afraid we wouldn't see the expected floral explosion on our adventure.

The longer we hiked, the fewer people we saw and the quieter the world became. It wasn't until our final descent that we turned a corner and my aching muscles and sore feet were temporarily forgotten. A sea of wildflowers burst forth in a hallelujah chorus in the fields around us.

Lavender lupines, magenta paintbrush wildflowers, and white daisies with bright yellow centers all stood tall and swayed in the gentle breeze. If this had been a musical, Maria from *The Sound of Music* would have been frolicking just around the bend, singing, "The hills are alive with the sound of music / With songs they have sung for a thousand years."[1] The hills were bursting with life, and the flowers were singing with reckless abandon.

The indescribable beauty of the moment overwhelmed my heart. Thousands upon thousands of wildflowers were growing all around us, and most would never be seen up close by a human eye. These wildflowers would grow, bloom, and die without ever being thanked by an onlooker or appreciated for their presence in the world. As I gazed at the beauties all around me, I whispered in my soul, *God, why did you make the wildflowers grow?*

WHY DID GOD MAKE WILDFLOWERS?

When a question like this sparks my interest, I don't stop digging until I find an answer. On our drive home (with ice cream in hand!), I started researching why wildflowers exist. Ralph Waldo Emerson creatively said, "Earth laughs in flowers."[2] And while it's true that wildflowers are an unparalleled delight, there's also purpose in each one, fashioned by the Designer of the flower himself.

Wildflowers do more for the world than just supply beauty, laughter, and a photo opportunity. Their unique designs, sweet fragrances, and punches of color make them excellent at attracting pollinators. According to the United States Department of Agriculture, wildflowers can "help boost crop yields, add natural proteins to the diets of livestock, provide erosion control on cropland, help manage and filter stormwater, create groundwater filtration systems and reduce the impacts of drought."[3] On top of all of that, around 35 percent of the world's food harvests are dependent on pollinators, which are drawn to wildflowers.[4] To bring it closer to home, the delicious meal you will enjoy today is due in part to wildflowers, which attracted pollinators, which in turn helped the crops grow.

What also amazes me is that every wildflower is different. No two are exactly alike, just as no two snowflakes or human beings are 100 percent identical. They all have their own mark of the Maker stamped on them. God didn't have to make the wildflowers explosions of beauty on top of all they do to help life flourish, but he did—and he did it on purpose.

CONSIDER THE WILDFLOWERS

In Luke 12:27-28, Jesus offers comfort to anxious hearts with this message of hope: "Consider how the wildflowers grow: They don't labor or spin thread. Yet I tell you, not even Solomon in all his splendor was adorned like one of these! If that's how God clothes the grass, which is in the field today and is thrown into the furnace tomorrow, how much more will he do for you—you of little faith?" (CSB). According to Jesus, big messages can be mined from these small beauties.

This passage is contained in the Sermon on the Mount, in which Jesus shared about the inside-out, upside-down ways of the Kingdom of God. Jesus' encouragement in this particular text is that we don't need to worry since we're cared for by the God of the universe.

People are a lot like wildflowers. Each one is different, each one is made on purpose, and each one has the potential to make a great impact on the world. But here's the catch: most of them will go unnoticed by people. Thousands of wildflowers blossom every year and are never seen, admired, or enjoyed by anyone but God. They just do what they were created to do. Their mission isn't to be recognized, applauded, or rewarded; their mission is to grow, drop their seeds, and do their small part in the bigger picture of creation. They don't compete or strive to be taller or more beautiful than their fellow wildflowers. They simply do what they were meant to do.

The same is true for you. Your life matters, and your mission isn't for tomorrow or "someday"—your mission is for right now.

Like the wildflowers, our efforts might go unnoticed by other people. But that's okay—and, dare I say, even a good thing.

"SOMEDAY" IS RIGHT NOW

Wildflowers don't live for "someday," when they might be admired or added to a bouquet and displayed in a vase. They grow under the sovereign care of God. They blossom for the glory of God. They flourish for the purposes of God. Wildflowers are good teachers to the anxious human heart that's always on the lookout for the next best thing. They teach us to trust in God's mighty purposes, to seek his eternal Kingdom, and to delight in his presence. Though their life span is short, they don't complain. They do what they were uniquely made to do.

I've often struggled with the temptation to live for "someday" instead of right now. When I was single, I was terrified God would call me to be an overseas missionary in some out-of-reach African jungle, where I'd be all alone and never meet my future husband. Instead, God called me to middle school ministry, where I met my future husband in the most unlikely of places (at middle school camp, where I was a counselor and he was working). When we got engaged, I was certain my life would be perfect once "Mrs." was added to my name.

But not much changed in my heart after we signed the marriage license and said "I do," so I kept looking to the next best thing. First, I looked forward to the day I could pursue my dream job, then to the day we would have kids (who would be perfect, of course), and then to the day we would have a lovely starter home. There's always something else on the horizon, luring us with a dangling promise of satisfaction, tempting us to miss out on the mission of God right now.

The more years I've lived on this earth, the more I'm convinced there's no perfect "someday." There is only *today*. There's only right now. The "someday" we hope for is eternity spent with him. Looking to eternity spurs us on to live faithfully and fully today.

After Jesus was raised from the dead and before his Ascension, he commissioned the disciples with these words: "All authority in heaven and on earth has been given to me. Go therefore and make disciples of all nations, baptizing them in the name of the Father and of the Son and of the Holy Spirit, teaching them to observe all that I have commanded you. And behold, I am with you always, to the end of the age" (Matthew 28:18-20).

The commission is clear: go and make disciples. This is a calling for us, too, even when we find ourselves in "imperfect" circumstances. Don't miss the joy and purpose of today by hoping for a better tomorrow. Proverbs 27:1 reminds us that we are not promised tomorrow (or even the end of today). What we have is this day, this moment.

Though our lives and day-to-day activities will look different from those of the first disciples, our mission is still the same: to know Christ and make him known. And that mission is for yesterday, today, and tomorrow.

Don't settle for less, sister. Christ came to give fullness, direction, and mission. Life apart from Christ is a life of less. When consumed with our own plans for our lives, we're left directionless, lifeless, and mission-less. But the more we live out the Great Commission right now, the more we long for what will truly satisfy us. We can live as wildflowers blooming at the perfect time, for the glory of God.

TRUST THE MAPMAKER

One month after Greg and I were married, we attended a missions conference where we met David Sitton, founder of To Every Tribe Missions. David Sitton is a missions pioneer who has committed to follow Jesus to the ends of the earth. In his book *Reckless Abandon*, he explains, "No special call was necessary. I chose to go. I wanted to go. . . . I was compelled to go. It was a privilege to go. Where I go is determined by an open

Bible and a stretched out map of locations that still needed to be pioneered for Jesus."[5]

In our brief conversation with him, we asked how we would know if we were going in the right direction and how we would get to the place God called us to be. As newlyweds, we were uncertain what our next step should be, and we desperately wanted to hear words of wisdom. David's response has been forever seared in my memory: "Keep going and trust God to get you to the right place."

That was it. The mission is already laid out in Scripture: go and make disciples. Go and share the Good News. Go and live like the Bible is true! Go—*today*.

What does this mean for the mama with a mountain of laundry waiting to be folded? For the college student searching for a job after graduation? For the single woman finding her footing in a life she didn't expect? For the woman stuck in a career she doesn't love? It means you consider the wildflowers that are growing where God planted them and doing what God made them to do—without caring about being noticed, just being obedient. You stay close to God in the Word, surrendering your plans and purposes to him and receiving his promise of peace and presence along the way. You put one foot in front of the other and take one step at a time to fulfill the gospel mission.

Just. One. Step.

Even if your life doesn't feel ideal, even if your fear is real, even if your feet stumble, even if your attempts crumble—you still move forward and trust the Mapmaker.

When we first started our hike up the Paradise trail, we had a small map to guide us. But it wasn't until we were actually walking, putting one foot in front of the other, that we got to where we wanted to be. We followed the winding trail up rocky mounts and down steep paths. We trusted as we walked, believing the path would take us to our destination. It did, and it was worth it.

What if following Jesus means living with gratitude for today instead of hoping for a better tomorrow?

What if instead of looking for "someday"—when you'll have a ring on your finger or a baby on your hip or an added credential on your résumé—you decided to use your tools, resources, and circumstances to know God more and make him known right now?

What if you stopped begging God for a GPS with detailed directions about the next five years and started applying the words of Scripture to your everyday life?

You don't have to have the perfect plan to be faithful today. God has the plan. He holds the map. We have his Word. That's more than enough.

IF NOT NOW, THEN WHEN?

When I was a preteen, I was what you might call a gel pen hoarder. I collected gel pens spanning the hues of the rainbow.

Some glittered, some shimmered, and some were clear with invisible ink (my favorite kind to write secret messages with in my journal). When I got a new set of pens, I made sure not to use them too much. They were so precious to me that I saved them in a special Crayola box, hidden from sight. I rarely enjoyed these pens to their full potential because I was too afraid of "wasting" them. (Because, apparently, I thought there would be a shortage at the store at some point.)

A few months ago, while visiting my parents, I found that Crayola box with my stash of gel pens! At more than twenty years old, a few of them still had a little bit of usable ink left, but most of them had dried up long ago. These precious pens weren't used and enjoyed when they were intended to be, and now they're useless.

Far too often, we do the same thing with the good gifts God has given us. We keep them tucked away for a future time and miss out on their purpose and enjoyment today. If we aren't faithful now, then when will we be? If we won't share Christ now, then when? If we won't bloom now, then what's today for?

God saved you for a mission and purpose right now, not someday. Remember the wildflowers, and bloom for the glory of God—even when you feel unseen.

THE WELL-WATERED WOMAN

DOESN'T PUT OFF LIVING

AS SHE WAITS FOR "SOMEDAY."

SHE KNOWS HER MISSION

IS NOW, AND SHE LIVES

WITH GOSPEL PURPOSE

GUIDING HER EVERY STEP.

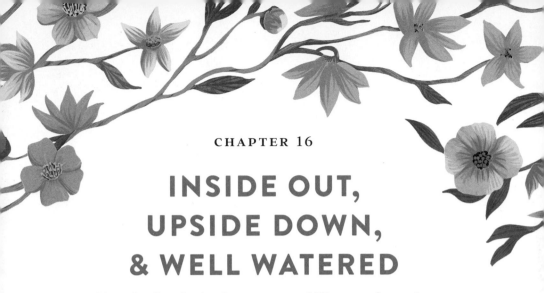

CHAPTER 16

INSIDE OUT, UPSIDE DOWN, & WELL WATERED

Live today for what is going to matter 10 billion years from today.

DAVID PLATT

The Story of a Well-Watered Woman

She started living life backwards, and everyone around her could see a difference. She looked people in the eye and listened intently to their stories. She didn't just tell people she would pray for them; she did it right away. She no longer read her Bible with a sense of duty; she read with sheer delight guiding her soul. She gave of her time, money, possessions, and talents. She shared her faith with anyone who would listen, she loved her neighbors, she opened her home, and she served her church any way she could. Though she didn't have much to offer by the world's standards, she gladly gave what she had to the one who gave everything for her. She never forgot what it was like to live the dried-up life, so she was forever grateful for the well-watered life she experienced each day in Jesus.

OUTSIDE MY WINDOW, the trees are budding and the flowers are blooming, waking from their slumber. After a long winter, I'm more than ready for this new season when the world bursts back to life.

While the trees and plants outside are on the verge of coming alive, on our kitchen table my long-awaited amaryllis has finally bloomed. Four cherry-red flowers grew from the bulb I planted after the loss of our baby. It took longer than I hoped, but each step along the way—the planting, the rooting, the growing, and the waiting—has led to the grand finale of blooming and flourishing.

Waiting for the flowers to bloom brought anticipation to my heart after a season of loss. Each day I looked forward to checking for signs of change. Through that process of slow growth, God showed me that sorrow and darkness don't last forever. Even in death, God can bring about new life.

EVERY MOMENT MATTERS

Life ebbs and flows in the rhythm of seasons. God, the Gardener of our souls, faithfully prunes, tends, weeds, and waters us to produce a harvest for his glory. There's meaning in the in-between moments, and there's mission in the ever-changing growth of our souls. Not a moment goes by that doesn't have eternal worth.

> Today's decisions affect tomorrow's destination.
> Today's faithfulness affects tomorrow's fruitfulness.
> Today's investment affects tomorrow's blooms.

You have everything you need to live a flourishing life in Christ (see Ephesians 1:3). This doesn't mean you'll always see or even feel the flourishing, but when your roots run deep and your foundation is built on the solid rock of Jesus Christ, the only possible result is a Spirit-led flourishing. This is something the world doesn't understand, but it's something it wants nonetheless.

In our quest for a fruitful life, it's important to remember that blooms aren't continuous. They come and go, but that doesn't mean the moments in between are unnecessary or less important. Blooms result from the faithful labor done in the planting, the rooting, the growing, and the waiting. You can't enjoy a flower without the long process that brought it to that point.

In my own life, I struggle to embrace the inside-out process of Christ-centered growth. It's easy to neglect the importance of the planting, the rooting, the growing, and the waiting. But the well-watered life isn't just one that blooms; it's one that's *always growing.* We strive to give glory to God at each stage, and we trust him with the harvest. Blooming will certainly come, but don't miss the joy and beauty of growing. Most of your life will be filled with normal, unrecorded, unexciting moments— and they *all* matter!

> The decisions you make today affect where you end up tomorrow.
> What you think about right now will impact who you will become.
> How you spend your time will determine the direction of your days.

The little moments matter more than we give them credit for. Instead of focusing on the blooming, let's strive to be faithful in the growing. And let's leave the rest in the hands of the Gardener.

WHEN BLOOMS ARE SLOW TO COME

Did you know that the actual blooming of some flowers can take *years*? Even when blooms aren't evident, there's still growth happening. This season of apparent dormancy doesn't negate the importance of the flower; it emphasizes the importance of the process.

There's a flower called the Queen of the Night that blooms only one night a year. Yes, you read that correctly: *one* night a year! The rest of the year it looks dead, but one night, in the summer heat, it opens up to reveal a breathtaking white flower. Then there's the giant Himalayan lily, which blooms every *seven* years. This massive plant grows up to ten feet tall before it blooms with beautiful bell-shaped lilies. After it blooms, it dies, leaving behind smaller bulbs so it can reproduce. The century plant blooms ten to twenty-five years after its initial planting. Once it's fully grown, it can reach almost thirty feet, with spiky green flowers, before it dies.[1]

Becoming a Well-Watered Woman for the glory of God doesn't happen by accident, and it won't happen overnight; it takes time, discipline, and surrender. It's an inside-out, upside-down process—and it's the way to abundant life.

The prophet Isaiah recorded an incredible promise to Israel: "The LORD will guide you always; he will satisfy your needs in a sun-scorched land and will strengthen your frame. You will be like a well-watered garden, like a spring whose waters never fail" (Isaiah 58:11, NIV). This is the kind of life I want, and it's what I desire for you, too.

It's helpful to consider the context of this passage as we think about its application for us. The surrounding verses are calling the people to turn from their false idols and meaning-less rituals to experience real worship of the one, true God. God was calling the Israelites out of their hypocrisy to a life of genuine faithfulness. The people were trying to flourish through their outward actions without having changed hearts, and God made it clear that this was not the life he called them to live.

The Lord sent this word to the Israelites through Isaiah:

Is not this the fast that I choose: to loose the bonds
of wickedness, to undo the straps of the yoke, to let
the oppressed go free, and to break every yoke? Is it
not to share your bread with the hungry and bring
the homeless poor into your house; when you see the
naked, to cover him, and not to hide yourself from
your own flesh?

ISAIAH 58:6-7

God flipped their lives upside down and showed them where true blessing comes from. It's not something that can be manufactured or manipulated; it comes only from his mighty work within our surrendered hearts. Ultimately, this is a picture of the Christian life, of the well-watered life.

BACKWARDS LIVING

From Genesis to Revelation, God calls his people to lives of authenticity, humility, and freedom—and this looks inside out and upside down compared to the ways of this world.

Jesus calls us to a life of backwards living. Isaiah 55:8-9 tells us that God's thoughts aren't our thoughts and our ways aren't his ways. Paul echoes this idea in 1 Corinthians 1:25: "The foolishness of God is wiser than human wisdom, and the weakness of God is stronger than human strength" (NIV). Even our best falls flat before the Lord (see Isaiah 64:6; Romans 3:10-12). His wisdom and his ways prevail over our plans, thoughts, and ideas. The ways of Christ don't always make sense to our finite minds, but we can trust that his ways are best. It's been proven since the dawn of time.

In the Sermon on the Mount, Jesus laid the foundation for true blessedness, which is precisely the opposite of what the world says: "Blessed are the poor in spirit, for theirs is the kingdom of heaven. Blessed are those who mourn, for they shall be comforted. Blessed are the meek, for they shall inherit the earth. Blessed are those who hunger and thirst for righteousness, for they shall be satisfied" (Matthew 5:3-6).

Then Jesus takes it even further: "Blessed are those who are persecuted for righteousness' sake, for theirs is the kingdom of heaven. . . . Rejoice and be glad, for your reward is great in heaven, for so they persecuted the prophets who were before you" (Matthew 5:10, 12). As Jesus teaches about the inside-out Kingdom of God, he upends every human notion.

Here are a few examples from this passage:

Jesus says that we shouldn't love just our neighbor; we should love our enemies (see Matthew 5:43-45).
Jesus says that faithfulness begins in secret, not in public (see Matthew 6:1).

Jesus says that we should forgive since we've been forgiven
by God (see Matthew 6:14).
Jesus says that we should store up treasures in heaven
rather than on earth (see Matthew 6:19-21).

I could keep going, but it's pretty clear that following Jesus
and enjoying the well-watered life means you're going to look
different from the rest of the world. The well-watered life is the
full, abundant, and free life, but it's also a countercultural life.

Paul describes believers this way: "We are fools for Christ's
sake, but you are wise in Christ. We are weak, but you are
strong. You are held in honor, but we in disrepute. . . . When
reviled, we bless; when persecuted, we endure; when slan-
dered, we entreat" (1 Corinthians 4:10, 12-13). Following Jesus
looks foolish to this world, but, sister, it's the way of abundance!
This is the life you were made to live, so don't settle for less.

NOT ONE-SIZE-FITS-ALL

A life of fruitfulness won't be easy, but it will be worth it.
Dietrich Bonhoeffer said, "When Christ calls a man, he bids
him come and die."[2] When Bonhoeffer said this, he didn't know
that following Jesus would lead to a martyr's death. But he also
didn't know his death would lead to spiritual life for many. His
life bloomed through hardship and persecution, and through
his death, it continues to reproduce for the glory of God.

When your life is offered to God, it can and will have

Kingdom impact. As you die daily to yourself, seeds will fall and produce a gospel harvest in the lives of others. Whether this is one person or one thousand, remember that just one life matters to God. Even if you're never seen or acknowledged for your faithfulness to Jesus, it will all still matter. That's a hope you can cling to each moment.

The well-watered life is not a one-size-fits-all formula. It's a calling to know Christ and make him known, and this calling manifests itself in the unique ways God has created you. Move forward seeking to know and love Jesus without comparing yourself to the people around you. Celebrate your sisters as they live out God's plan for them. Keep your gaze on the Cross. And remember that one day you will lay a crown at the feet of Jesus, who is worthy of your every breath (see James 1:12; 1 Peter 5:4; Revelation 4:10-11).

ENDLESS WAYS TO LIVE WELL WATERED

There are as many ways to live a well-watered life as there are people. God is infinitely creative, and he can cause us to flourish in any environment, under any circumstances. Here are just a few snapshots of what the Well-Watered Woman may look like in real life. These women from different backgrounds reflect his grace in the midst of their struggles and his strength in their life challenges. They are all sinners saved by grace who are seeking to live out their faith in everything they do.

The well-watered life looks like my Mawmaw, Jenny Pitt,

who had crippling rheumatoid arthritis and used a wheelchair for most of her life. Still, she lifted her disfigured hands in worship and surrender to God. Every person who came into contact with her saw Christ shine through her suffering. As her disability worsened, she was no longer able to open her Bible by herself, but the Word of God continued to dwell in her spirit.

It looks like my mama, Kathy, whose life has also been fraught with physical pain as she battles a rare autoimmune disease. Even when she was at her lowest point physically, unable to see or to walk on her own, she sought the Lord and shared about him with her nurses. She taught me how to pray with honesty and boldness, knowing God is faithful to hear and answer us.

It looks like my sister, Kara, who after years of infertility became pregnant and gave birth to a little girl named Kate, and then years later was surprised with another pregnancy. At fourteen weeks, her second daughter was diagnosed with Down syndrome. Around the same time, Kara and her husband adopted a little boy from the foster care system. Every day, Kara navigates the unique challenges of caring for her three children, two of whom need developmental therapy. Her life looks different from what she expected, but she hands God the pen to write the narrative of her days.

It looks like Mrs. Carla, my mentor and pastor's wife when I was in college, who welcomed girls into her home every week and shared Jesus with us. She raised five children while helping her husband and serving the local church body, in addition to nurturing the souls of many brokenhearted young women who spent time with her. Her humility and graciousness point to her Savior and Sustainer, Jesus.

It looks like Meredith, a sister in Christ I met online, who cuts and colors hair for the glory of God, praying for her clients and showing them where true beauty is ultimately found—in knowing our identity in Jesus Christ.

It looks like my friend Ali, who has had a passion for running since high school. God continues to use her ability to run marathons to provide her with opportunities to share her faith, shape her own heart, and spend time praying for her friends.

It looks like my friend Jessica, who moved to Mexico in her early twenties to serve as a teacher to missionary kids. After her years overseas, she moved back to her college town as a single woman longing to be married, but she resolved to be faithful to Jesus no matter what. While she served at an inner city school, she met her now husband, and today she continues to share the love of Jesus as a foster mama and through serving in various local ministries.

It looks like Ayanna, who works at a local mall while also faithfully serving at her local church and blogging about biblical womanhood. Though she isn't in full-time ministry, she views her entire life as an opportunity to minister to others, to be a disciple, and to make disciples.

It looks like Natalie, who went to medical school so she could become a physician and help care for the broken, hurting, and wounded. After years of study, she now works at a hospital, loving people in their vulnerable state, living as a light for Jesus.

Ultimately, the Well-Watered Woman looks like *you*, right where you are as you seek Jesus. You won't do everything perfectly—God already knows that. That's why he sent his perfect Son to die in your place. You are in process, but God sees the end result. Trust him with the moments in between. Change is happening, and blooms are coming, but abiding and flourishing can happen right now, right where you are.

THE UNWASTED LIFE

Jesus calls us to an unwasted life—a well-watered life. In his book *Don't Waste Your Life*, John Piper says, "Whatever you do, find the God-centered, Christ-exalting, Bible-saturated passion of your life, and find your way to say it and live for it and die for it. And you will make a difference that lasts. You will not waste your life."[3] This is what I want, for you and for myself, and this is what God wants for us.

The unwasted life is a paradox, a mystery to the human soul. This prayer summarizes the inside-out, upside-down life with raw honesty:

Let me learn by paradox
That the way down is the way up,
That to be low is to be high,

That the broken heart is the healed heart,
That the contrite spirit is the rejoicing spirit,
That the repenting soul is the victorious soul,
That to have nothing is to possess all,
That to bear the cross is to wear the crown,
That to give is to receive,
That the valley is the place of vision.[4]

We usually try to avoid the valley because we are afraid of what we will endure in the low moments of life when the darkness closes in. But the valley holds the sweetest fruit, the brightest flowers, and the greenest grass. The valley is where growth happens. The valley is part of every journey, and it typically follows every mountaintop moment. I tell you this because I want to set your expectations straight. You won't have your life completely figured out after you've finished reading this book. But you will, I hope, have your gaze fixed on Jesus and your confidence focused on his Word. And that will get you through any high or low, any drought or storm, any desert or mountain trail.

THE WELL-WATERED GARDEN TO COME

This is just another beginning in the middle of your story. While humanity's story began in a garden, it will culminate in another Garden—a perfect, redeemed, everlasting, always-blooming Garden.

In the Garden of Eden, sin broke its innocent perfection (see Genesis 3). But the Gardener and Creator of all things didn't leave us without hope. He began a work of redemption that's woven throughout the entire Bible, in what has been and in what is to come. When Jesus came in God's perfect timing, he broke the curse of sin by dying in our place on a tree (see Galatians 3:13). He didn't stay in the grave, though. He shattered the darkness and rose again.

But this is not the end. As Christians redeemed by the blood of Jesus, we look with hope to the day Jesus will come again for his people. When he comes, he will defeat Satan, finally and forever (see Revelation 12). Satan, the author of all lies and accuser of all people, will be crushed, no longer able to plant weeds or wreak havoc in the Garden of God. As Well-Watered Women, we keep in mind the glorious Garden to come.

Jesus, who is the Well of living water, the Word of freedom, and the Way of fruitfulness will reign in the glorious, well-watered Garden, and we will spend eternity worshiping and serving him. We will behold him fully, and his name will be written on our foreheads, never to be erased (see Revelation 22:4). No longer will our identity roots be tangled with lies. No longer will the weeds of sin threaten to destroy us. No longer will we harvest rotten fruit. No longer will we languish, struggle, toil, and encounter trouble. We will enjoy the fruit of the glory of God as we drink deeply of the living water forever and ever (see John 4:14; Revelation 22:1).

The Curse will be reversed, darkness will cease, and there won't even be a need for light because Jesus himself will be the Light (see Revelation 22:5). Every month the tree of life will bear fruit, never dying, never rotting (see Revelation 22:2). This is the true and better Garden, the one Jesus is preparing you for as you walk through dark valleys, climb steep mountains, and endure dry deserts. This is your hope, and this is your future.

Live for the eternal, well-watered Garden to come as you embrace every moment in the middle.

THE WELL-WATERED WOMAN

EMBRACES THE ETERNAL,

BACKWARDS WAY

OF THE KINGDOM OF GOD,

WILLING TO STICK OUT

IN THIS WORLD

FOR JESUS' SAKE.

The Well-Watered Woman
STATEMENTS

Now that you've finished reading the book, take a moment to review each Well-Watered Woman statement. Remember, the journey isn't over; it has just begun! Read through these statements any time you need a refresher about what it means to live the well-watered life as you continue to grow in grace each day.

The Well-Watered Woman surrenders a life of striving for a life of sinking her roots into God's Word.

The Well-Watered Woman knows who Jesus is, and who he is changes everything about her past, present, and future.

The Well-Watered Woman meets Jesus at the grace well and exchanges her nothing for his everything.

The Well-Watered Woman is planted in the soil of the gospel, and, like a seed buried in the earth, she embraces death as the means to abundant life.

*The Well-Watered Woman recognizes that true joy doesn't come
from coffee, vacation, naps, success, or comfort.
Her joy comes only from the Lord.*

---

*The Well-Watered Woman trusts the mysterious ways of God,
knowing he has a purpose for where she's planted.*

---

*The Well-Watered Woman resolves to get nourishment
from the one source that truly satisfies: the Word of God.*

---

*The Well-Watered Woman allows the Holy Spirit to burn away
the chaff of her life to clear the way for a mighty work of God.*

---

*The Well-Watered Woman abides in Christ and recognizes
that apart from him, she can do nothing.*

---

*The Well-Watered Woman stores the Word in her heart, knowing
that God has provided everything she needs to grow, bloom,
and flourish even in the midst of the desert seasons.*

---

*The Well-Watered Woman takes her wayward thoughts captive,
conforming them to the ways of Jesus.*

---

*The Well-Watered Woman embraces sanctification,
knowing it's the only path to flourishing.*

*The Well-Watered Woman follows Jesus wholeheartedly, knowing
that in order to lead well, she must first be a disciple of Jesus.*

*The Well-Watered Woman looks for gospel intersections
in her everyday life, knowing that even
the mundane matters in the Kingdom of God.*

*The Well-Watered Woman doesn't put off living as she waits
for "someday." She knows her mission is now,
and she lives with gospel purpose guiding her every step.*

*The Well-Watered Woman embraces the eternal, backwards way of the
Kingdom of God, willing to stick out in this world for Jesus' sake.*

ACKNOWLEDGMENTS

First and foremost, to my Savior, my God, my King: You are my best friend, my Redeemer, my everything. This book would not exist apart from your saving grace. There were many times I wanted to give up, but you helped me press in and press on. I am living proof that you can take a broken life and make it brand new. This is for you, because of you, and all for your glory.

To my husband, Greg: No one will see how much you sacrificed to make this book possible. You prayed for me when I was weak, encouraged me when I was discouraged, and spoke words of life into me every step of the way. You humbly serve our family, and you show me what it means to love like Christ. I love you more than words can say!

To my family: You have loved me at my lowest and showed me the grace of Jesus. Mama, *you* are the Well-Watered Woman. What people don't know is that most of what I've written I learned from watching you. Thank you for reading the words of this book before anyone else did and for always pointing me back to Christ. Daddy, you have taught me what it looks like to trust the Lord, and you know just the right words to say in my moment of need. Thank you for believing in me and praying for me! Kara, my sees, I have always looked up to you, and you have always shown me that Jesus is worthy of my trust and my life. Thank you for faithfully leading me back to him! Jason, you are truly the best big brother. Thank you for always cheering me on and caring for me!

To my sweet boys, Nolan and Haddon: Your mama loves you so much! You bring joy to my heart every day and teach me what truly matters most in life. I praise God for both of you and pray you will treasure him all the days of your life.

To the Tyndale team: You truly practice what you preach. Your desire is to share the gospel and to love God wholeheartedly, and I am honored to work alongside you. Kara, you are more than an editor; you are a faithful friend and the best cheerleader! Thank you for loving me just as I am and encouraging me every step of the way! Stephanie, it has been an absolute joy to work with you! Your heart for the Word is reflected in all you say and do. Thank you for speaking God's truth into my life and for making this book a reflection of his heart! Libby, Dean, and Jillian, you worked so hard to make this book reflect the beauty of the Word through your design genius! And Teresa, you are truly a gift from God! You are more than a literary agent; you are my sister in Christ, and your heart for this book and message has inspired me to keep pursuing the Lord with all my heart!

To the Well-Watered Women team: Each one of you means more to me than you'll ever know. Thank you for praying for me and encouraging me! I am abundantly grateful for each one of you!

To my church family, my dear friends, and the many mentors who have walked with me at various points in life: You are all pictures of God's grace and reminders of his enduring love. The Lord has used all of you to show me the glorious gift of the gospel! This book is a testament that God works through people. Whitney and Madelyn, you have both walked with me since elementary school and have sharpened me and always stuck by my side! To my high school English teacher, Mr. Klempner, you challenged me to write creatively at a young age and honed those skills (even when I complained about your grammar tests!). Thank you for training me to be a writer when I didn't know I would be a writer.

Lastly, to Pawpaw and Mawmaw: I can't wait for the day I get to hug you both again in heaven. I was privileged to stand by both of your sides when you breathed your last breath, and those holy moments showed me there is more to life than this fleeting world. You taught me that suffering is not God's absence but a picture of his presence and his redemption. Your legacies are still alive and well, pointing people to our Savior, Jesus.

NOTES

CHAPTER 1: I'M NOT OKAY. IS THAT OKAY?
1. "8414. tohu," *Strong's Concordance*, accessed July 23, 2020, https://biblehub.com/hebrew/8414.htm.
2. Charles Haddon Spurgeon, "Thorns and Thistles," *Metropolitan Tabernacle Pulpit* 39, no. 2299 (March 12, 1893).
3. Nancy Guthrie, "Heaven Will Be Better Than Eden," September 1, 2018, Desiring God, https://www.desiringgod.org/articles/heaven-will-be-better-than-eden.

CHAPTER 2: IDENTITY ROOTS
1. Charles P. Stone, Clifford W. Smith, and J. Timothy Tunison, eds., *Alien Plant Invasions in Native Ecosystems of Hawai'i: Management and Research* (Honolulu: University of Hawaii Cooperative National Park Resources Study Unit, 1992), 193.

CHAPTER 4: DYING TO LIVE
1. I. Lilias Trotter, *Parables of the Cross* (The Project Gutenberg: 2007), e-book.
2. "3498. nekros," *Strong's Concordance*, accessed July 29, 2020, https://biblehub.com/greek/3498.htm.
3. Elisabeth Elliot, *A Chance to Die: The Life and Legacy of Amy Carmichael* (Ada, MI: Revell, 1987), 15.

CHAPTER 5: FORSAKING BROKEN WELLS
1. Study note for Jeremiah 2:12-13, *ESV Study Bible* (Wheaton, IL: Crossway, 2008), 1372.
2. C. S. Lewis, *The Weight of Glory* (New York: Harper Collins, 2001), 26.
3. F. B. Meyer, *Jeremiah: Priest and Prophet* (London: Morgan and Scott), 29, https://archive.org/stream/jeremiahpriestpr00meye#page/29/mode/1up/search/What+an+infinite+mistake+.
4. Steven Lawson, "William Tyndale's Final Words," Ligonier Ministries, February 18, 2015, https://www.ligonier.org/blog/william-tyndales-final-words/.
5. Bruce Hindmarsh, "Was He Too Prone to Wander? Robert Robinson (1735-1790)," Desiring God, June 16, 2019, https://www.desiringgod.org/articles/was-he-too-prone-to-wander.
6. F. B. Meyer, *Jeremiah: Priest and Prophet* (Fort Washington, PA: CLC, 2013), e-book.

CHAPTER 6: ANYWHERE BUT HERE
1. Elisabeth Elliot, *Through Gates of Splendor* (Carol Stream, IL: Tyndale, 1981), 20.

CHAPTER 7: WORD BEFORE WORLD
1. Tony Reinke, *12 Ways Your Phone Is Changing You* (Wheaton, IL: Crossway, 2017), 15.
2. For more on this concept, see Andy Crouch, *The Tech-Wise Family: Everyday Steps for Putting Technology in Its Proper Place* (Grand Rapids, MI: Baker Books, 2017), 18.
3. Stephen J. Nichols, "The Resolutions of Jonathan Edwards," *Tabletalk*, January 2009, https://tabletalkmagazine.com/article/2009/01/resolutions-jonathan -edwards/.
4. Jonathan Edwards, "Resolutions," *Works of Jonathan Edwards Online, Volume 16* (Jonathan Edwards Center, Yale University, 2008), 753, accessed on July 23, 2020.
5. Edwards, "Resolutions," 753.
6. Michael W. Smith, vocalist, "Ancient Words," 2002, by Lynn DeShazo (lyricist), track 4, on *Worship Again* (New York: Zoomba Recording, 2003), compact disc.
7. Smith, "Ancient Words."

CHAPTER 8: SPRINGING UP FROM THE ASHES
1. Laurie L. Dove, "How Does a Forest Fire Benefit Living Things?" HowStuffWorks.com, April 22, 2013, https://science.howstuffworks.com/environmental/green-science /how-forest-fire-benefit-living-things-2.htm.
2. Matt Chandler, "Stirring Your Affections for Jesus" (sermon), Bethlehem Baptist Church, St. Paul, MN, February 4, 2009, Desiring God, 18:24–18:27, https:// www.desiringgod.org/messages/stirring-your-affections-for-jesus.
3. Brother Lawrence, *The Practice of the Presence of God: The Best Rule of Holy Life* (Peabody, MA: Hendrickson, 2011), 98.
4. "Brother Lawrence: Practitioner of God's Presence," *Christianity Today*, accessed on July 23, 2020, https://www.christianitytoday.com/history/people/innertravelers /brother-lawrence.html.
5. Chandler, "Stirring Your Affections," 18:31–18:36.
6. Donald S. Whitney, *Spiritual Disciplines for the Christian Life* (Carol Stream, IL: Tyndale House Publishers, 2014), 50.
7. Thomas Watson, *Gleanings from Thomas Watson*, compiled by Hamilton Smith (Morgan, PA: Soli Deo Gloria, 1995), 106, 112.
8. David W. Saxton, *God's Battle Plan for the Mind: The Puritan Practice of Biblical Meditation* (Grand Rapids, MI: Reformation Heritage Books, 2015), 61.

CHAPTER 9: THE ART OF ABIDING
1. "3306. menó," *Strong's Concordance*, accessed on July 27, 2020, https:// biblehub.com/greek/3306.htm.
2. L. B. Cowman, *Streams in the Desert*, ed. James Reimann (Grand Rapids, MI: Zondervan, 1997), 305.
3. "1510. eimi," *Strong's Concordance*, accessed on July 27, 2020, https:// biblehub.com/greek/1510.htm.
4. "The True Vine," *Tabletalk*, January 2004, https://tabletalkmagazine.com/daily-study /2004/01/true-vine/.
5. Joe Rigney, *The Things of Earth: Treasuring God by Enjoying His Gifts* (Wheaton, IL: Crossway, 2014), 110.
6. George Müeller, *The Autobiography of George Müeller* (Dallas: Gideon House Books, 2017), 124.
7. John Piper, *Don't Waste Your Life* (Wheaton, IL: Crossway, 2007), 49.

8. Warren W. Wiersbe, *He Walks with Me: Enjoying the Abiding Presence of God* (Colorado Springs: David C. Cook, 2016), 143.

CHAPTER 10: IN EVERY SEASON
1. Rebekah Shaffer, "How Do Cacti Survive in That Environment?" ScienceIQ.com, accessed June 28, 2020, http://www.scienceiq.com/facts/cactisurvive.cfm.
2. Robert J. Morgan, *Then Sings My Soul: 150 of the World's Greatest Hymn Stories* (Nashville: Thomas Nelson Publishers, 2003), 283.
3. C. S. Lewis, *God in the Dock: Essays on Theology and Ethics*, ed. Walter Hooper (Grand Rapids, MI: Eerdmans, 1970), 310.

CHAPTER 11: A LIFELONG BATTLE
1. "342. anakainósis," *Strong's Concordance*, accessed July 15, 2020, https://biblehub.com/greek/342.htm.
2. Elyse M. Fitzpatrick, *Because He Loves Me: How Christ Transforms Our Daily Life* (Wheaton, IL: Crossway, 2008), 75–76.
3. David Martyn Lloyd-Jones, *Spiritual Depression: Its Causes and Its Cure* (Grand Rapids, MI: Eerdmans, 1965), 20.

CHAPTER 12: WEEDING OUT SIN
1. Nichole Nordeman, vocalist, "River God," 1998, by Nichole Nordeman (lyricist), track 12, on *The Ultimate Collection* (Brentwood, TN: Sparrow, 2009), compact disc.
2. Elisabeth Elliot, "Suffering Is Not for Nothing," ElisabethElliot.org, June 16, 2015, https://elisabethelliot.org/resource-library/talks/suffering-is-not-for-nothing-talk/.
3. Josh Linkner, "Why You Must Always 'Mind the Gap' in Your Personal and Professional Life," *Inc.*, February 9, 2016, https://www.inc.com/josh-linkner/mind-the-gap.html.
4. W. Duncan Rankin, "Being and Becoming," *Tabletalk*, May 2010, https://tabletalkmagazine.com/article/2010/05/being-and-becoming/.
5. Jerry Bridges, *The Pursuit of Holiness* (Colorado Springs: NavPress, 1978), 21.
6. Ruth Chou Simons, *Gracelaced: Discovering Timeless Truth through Seasons of the Heart* (Eugene, OR: Harvest House, 2017), 10.
7. Jerry Bridges, *The Pursuit of Holiness* (Colorado Springs: NavPress, 1978), 104.
8. "This Date in History: June 14, 2007—Remembering Ruth Bell Graham," Billy Graham Library, June 14, 2012, https://billygrahamlibrary.org/this-date-in-history-june-14-2007-remembering-ruth-bell-graham/.

CHAPTER 13: LEAD LIKE A FOLLOWER
1. Francis Chan, "Francis Chan on Leadership: Why It's So Easy for Leaders to Fake It," *Church Leaders*, October 18, 2014, https://churchleaders.com/pastors/pastor-articles/143491-public-passion-vs-private-devotion.html.

CHAPTER 14: GOSPEL INTERSECTIONS
1. Stephen Alexander, "20 years ago tonight. . . . It still seems like yesterday. I can only imagine what my Dad and Mom are doing right now," Facebook, December 30, 2019, https://www.facebook.com/stephen.alexander.311/posts/2412579592202882.
2. Learn more about Karen Alexander-Doyel at https://womensministry.lifeway.com/2019/10/14/remembering-karen-alexander-doyel/.
3. Robby Galatty, "The Forgotten Jesus Part 2: Was Jesus a Carpenter or a Stonemason?," Lifeway Leadership, accessed July 18, 2020, https://leadership.lifeway.com/2017/04/04/the-forgotten-jesus-part-2-was-jesus-a-carpenter-or-a-stonemason/.

4. Note for John 13:1-17, *ESV Study Bible* (Wheaton, IL: Crossway, 2008), 2050.
5. Elisabeth Elliot, *A Lamp unto My Feet: The Bible's Light for Your Daily Walk* (Grand Rapids, MI: Revell, 1985), 36.
6. Chris Adams, "Karen's Legacy," *Chris Adams* (blog), September 16, 2019, https://chrisadams.blog/2019/09/16/karens-legacy/.

CHAPTER 15: YOUR MISSION IS NOW
1. Julie Andrews, vocalist, "The Sound of Music . . . The Children and the Captain," 1965, by Oscar Hammerstein II (lyricist), track 9, on *The Sound of Music* (New York: RCA, 2000), compact disc.
2. Ralph Waldo Emerson, "Hamatreya," Poetry Foundation, https://www.poetryfoundation.org/poems/52341/hamatreya.
3. Jocelyn Benjamin, "Wildflowers Benefit Agricultural Operations, Ecosystems," USDA Natural Resources Conservation Service, May 1, 2017, https://www.nrcs.usda.gov/wps/portal/nrcs/detail/national/newsroom/features/?cid=NRCSEPRD1326644.
4. Benjamin, "Wildflowers."
5. David Sitton, *Reckless Abandon* (Greenville, SC: Ambassador International, 2011), 47.

CHAPTER 16: INSIDE OUT, UPSIDE DOWN, AND WELL WATERED
1. Sal Vaglica, "8 Exotic Plants That Take Up to a Decade—or More—to Bloom," *This Old House*, September 15, 2015, https://www.thisoldhouse.com/gardening/21018053/8-exotic-plants-that-take-up-to-a-decade-or-more-to-bloom.
2. Dietrich Bonhoeffer, *The Cost of Discipleship* (New York: Touchstone, 1995), 89.
3. John Piper, *Don't Waste Your Life* (Wheaton, IL: Crossway, 2003), 57.
4. Arthur Bennett, ed., *The Valley of Vision*, (Carlisle, PA: Banner of Truth Trust, 1975), xv.

ABOUT THE AUTHOR

GRETCHEN SAFFLES is the founder of the global online women's ministry Well-Watered Women, the creator of the *Give Me Jesus* quiet time journal, and a passionate writer who longs to see women grasp the fullness of the gospel in everyday life. As a wife and mama, Gretchen has learned firsthand that just because your hands and days are full doesn't mean that your heart has to be empty. As she shares from her life experiences, Gretchen writes with authenticity and boldness, encouraging women to seek Christ right where they are and live in his abundance.

Her journey into ministry started after college when she began working in women's ministry at a church in Nashville. God used this experience as a training ground to grow her love for women, and he gave her a passion for seeing both women and girls live deeply rooted in God's Word. After she married Greg and moved to Knoxville, Tennessee, she took a leap of faith and began an online shop and ministry called Life Lived

Beautifully. Having no idea where else to start, she began right where she was, with what she had: a small amount of savings, a prayer journal, and a big dream stirring deep within her soul to encourage women to love Jesus deeply.

In 2014, God planted a seed in Gretchen's heart to create a quiet time journal for women to study God's Word. Through a series of God-ordained circumstances, the first *Give Me Jesus* journal launched in May of that year. Since then, Gretchen's mission has been to create quiet time journals, Bible study tools, and gospel-centered content that stirs women's affections for Christ and equips them to know him more through his Word.

Gretchen changed the name of the ministry to Well-Watered Women in 2016 to encompass its goal and mission based on Isaiah 58:11. Over the years, Gretchen has self-published several Bible studies, sold updated and revised versions of the *Give Me Jesus* journal, and created other guided journals and resources that walk women through various books of the Bible. She has a degree in fashion merchandising from the University of Georgia and loves to creatively show women they have been made in the image of God to reflect and enjoy him.

Gretchen lives in Atlanta with Greg and their two sons, Nolan and Haddon. Gretchen loves going on adventures with her family, traveling to new places, daydreaming of wildflower fields, cooking tasty meals, baking chocolate chip cookies, painting, reading good books, and teaching women to know and love Jesus.

For more information on Well-Watered Women, visit the Well-Watered Women website and stay in touch through their social media pages. You can also follow Gretchen on Instagram.

- WWW.WELLWATEREDWOMEN.COM
- WELLWATEREDWOMEN
- @WELLWATEREDWOMEN
- @GRETCHENSAFFLES
- @WELLWATEREDCO